Dedication

I would like to thank Lil' Dude for reminding me that life is all about taking walks, finding a good snack, and making time for an occasional afternoon nap.

My four-footed friend is often wiser than I give him credit for.

Understanding Paul's Epistle to the

Colossians

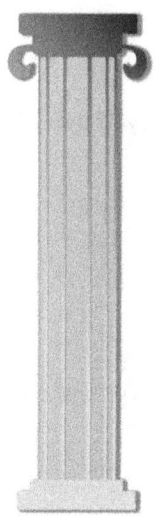

Farley Dunn

Understanding Paul's Epistle to the Colossians/Farley Dunn – 2nd ed.

COPYRIGHT © 2014 BY FARLEY DUNN

www.mychurchnotes.net

All rights reserved

ISBN: 978-1-943189-14-4

THREE SKILLET
www.ThreeSkilletPublishing.com

Contents

Paul's Time Is Now	9
Identity Confirmed	15
A Thanksgiving Feast	25
Brain Freeze	35
No Lifeguard on Duty	41
Trading Stamp Redemption	51
God's Glass Menagerie	59
Jesus in Focus	69
Simon Says	79
The Wall of Honor	89
Blinded by Fog	99
Blowing Out the Candle	109
1-800-GOJESUS	119
Planting October's Spring Garden	131
Scraping the Paint	139
Putting on the Ritz	147
The Weaving Machine	159
Tit for Tat	169
Broken Rope	179
Refer-a-Friend	187
Tarmac Touchdown	197

Paul's Time Is Now

Introduction

When Paul wrote his epistle to the church at Colosse, he wrote to his contemporaries in ordinary, everyday language that they understood. In his references, his analogies, and even his allegories, there was nothing he said that would have been unclear to those who read his writings.

We forget that Paul did not write in King James English, New American Standard, or even the much-loved and oft-quoted New International Version.

Paul wrote in Greek, a language unfamiliar to much of the modern English-speaking world, but one that was widely used in his day. Phrases that we look to Bible linguists to explain, such as "putting off the body of the sins of the flesh" and "For ye are dead, and your life is hid with Christ in God," were understood as ordinary, everyday allusions to the people who received Paul's writings. Of course even that is misleading, because these were phrases in popular use fifteen centuries after Paul's death.

To understand Paul's intent in using the words and phrases he did, and to apply his words and meanings to our lives today, we have to couch his words in modern-day concepts. Paul wrote in phrases and concepts his contemporaries understood, and we have to read his writings in terms we understand.

For example, in the 21st century we might say that someone bought the farm. That phrase can have several meanings, from the literal one indicating a monetary purchase, to a colloquial one meaning to pass on after death.

If we are involved in a dangerous situation, we might even have someone say to us, "You try it, and it's your farm."

They are saying that the risk is ours, and we face the possibility of death if we continue.

But do we know where that phrase originated?

In the early 20th century, many soldiers came from a farming background. While military pay was low, the U.S. government would compensate families for soldiers' deaths. The ensuing check would often "buy the farm," or pay off the mortgage on the family farm.

Meanings of common terms, such as "go for the brass ring" and "balls to the wall," have also changed over the years. Eventually the original meaning is lost, and we only generally understand what the phrase might have originally meant.

If we say "go for the brass ring" now, we mean to go for the top job or to aim our expectations high.

Go for the brass ring was originally a phrase from old carousel rides, where the riders grabbed metal rings as they passed by an elevated stand. Every tenth or hundredth ring was brass. Grab it, and we won the grand prize.

To say "balls to the wall" in modern terminology means to put everything we've got into what we're doing; to make an all-out effort.

Balls to the wall was originally a mechanical term meaning to push the throttle to maximum speed until the governor (either the centrifugal balls on early steam engines or the hand-held throttle in early aircraft) hits the wall, forcing the engine to go at the maximum speed possible.

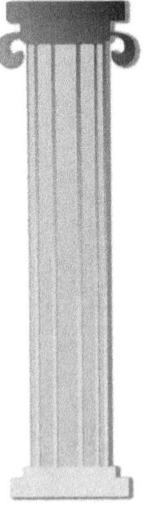

A hundred years ago, everyone in American culture would have understood those common, everyday phrases. Now, no one understands them in their original context. They have become idioms, words that mean something other than what they really say.

If those phrases have changed that much after one hundred years, how much have Paul's writings changed in two thousand years? We no longer understand his idioms or the cultural context in which he wrote.

We must look at Paul's writings in the context of our modern world.

Paul's time is now, and this book will help you understand what the believers at Colosse understood his words to mean.

This is Paul speaking to us in 21st century language.

You will enjoy the Epistle of Paul to the Colossians as you never have before.

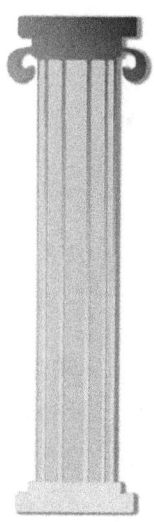

Identity Confirmed

Colossians 1:1-2

A spy's true strength is in his anonymity. He must be able to step into any situation, complete his assignment, and step out again, never recognized for exactly who he is.

He must be able to disappear into the woodwork, to be swallowed into the crowd, to become invisible against a sea of faces.

Yet, when he contacts his superiors, he must be clearly identifiable, leaving no doubt that he is who he says he is. The spy must be able to prove he is who he claims to be.

Paul was a man of many faces. Oh, we do not see him that way now, for we have had two thousand years to define just who this man was. However, in A.D. 64, he was still living out the life of the person we now know as one of the greatest Apostles of all time.

Paul's contemporaries did not have the advantage of two millennia to give them the perspective we have today. **Paul was under pressure to make his identity clear each and every time he communicated with his fellow believers.** In Colossians 1:1, Paul begins his epistle by laying out his credentials in three clear proofs.

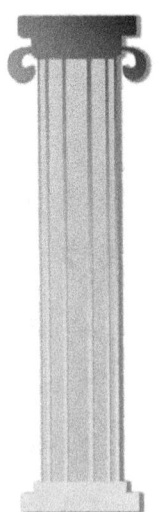

Identity Proof #1: Paul, an Apostle of Jesus Christ . . .

To us, with millennia of hindsight at our disposal, this statement is obvious. However, in the Early Church, this was not accepted by everyone. Paul had to make his position clear. The church is led by the Holy Spirit. Paul had received the revelation of grace through the

Spirit, and it was through this authority that he could lead the church.

Identity Proof #2: Through the Will of God . . .

The early Christians were often generous in supporting the burgeoning church. A wandering "prophet" could make good money pretending to share the Word of God.

However, only God could place a person into the office of prophet or apostle. Man did not have the authority to do so.

Paul wanted the proof of his authority to be God.

Identity Proof #3: And Timothy our Brother . . .

Timothy was a much younger companion to Paul, one who had been very beneficial in Paul's ministry. To associate himself with Timothy was to gain approval from those who knew and appreciated Timothy's ministry.

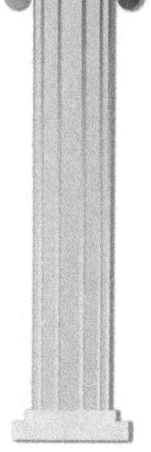

Paul didn't stop there. As a spy must identify himself to his superiors, so must the spy confirm the identity of those to whom he reports. Hence, Colossians 1:2, in which Paul also lays out the identity of those to whom he writes in three clear confirmations.

Identity Confirmation #1: To the Saints . . .

This phrase is a clear indication of one thing. Paul had no doubt of the heart of the Colossian brethren. Paul recognized in his words that the moment a person accepts Christ, he becomes a saint. There is no delay, no proving of "miracles," no wait time after the person dies. The acceptance of Jesus makes one a saint.

Identity Confirmation #2: And Faithful Brethren in Christ . . .

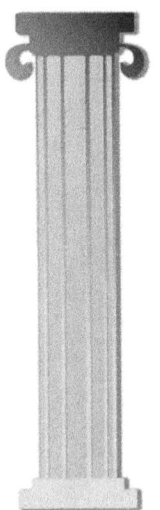

Paul was not blind. Not all those in the body at Colosse were as invested in their Christian walk as others. Paul was writing to the faithful among the church.

Identify Confirmation #3: Which are at Colosse . . .

This epistle was written for one body,

and one only. The needs of the believers were (and are) very specific, and Paul was attuned to the individual. He knew that the message of Christ was not one-fits-all.

What the Colossian body needed to hear was vastly different than what the Corinthians needed. Paul introduced his letter as such, letting the people know just whom he was writing to.

Finally, Paul could greet his audience. They knew exactly where he stood, and he had called them out for exactly who they were.

The business side of his introductions was cleared out of the way, and the real message could start.

> "Grace be unto you, and peace,
> from God our Father and the
> Lord Jesus Christ."

Paul knew where his strength lay.

It flowed from the Name of the Father, the Son, and the Spirit. Without them, he had no identity at all, and his life was worthless.

In summary, when God confirms our

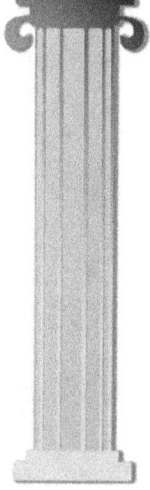

identity, we become someone of incalculable worth.

Amen.

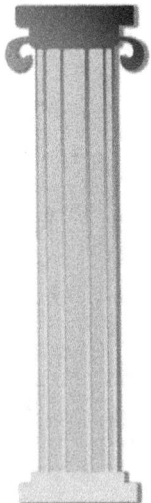

Read about it in the Bible:

Colossians 1:1-2 (KJV)

> Paul, an apostle of Jesus Christ by the will of God, and Timotheus our brother, to the saints and faithful brethren in Christ which are at Colosse: Grace be unto you, and peace, from God our Father and the Lord Jesus Christ.

Identity Confirmed

Questions for Group Discussion

1. Why did the people of Paul's day have so much trouble accepting his role in the Early Church?

   _____

   _____

   _____

2. Do people have trouble accepting us as Christ's servants today? Why or why not?

   _____

   _____

   _____

3. If you chose someone to verify your role in the body of Christ, who would that be?

   _____

   _____

   _____

4. How can other Christians recognize Christ's workings in your life?

_____

_____

_____

5. List three things you expect to see in Christians around you, things that identify them as followers of Christ, not just as members of a church.

_____

_____

_____

A Thanksgiving Feast

Colossians 1:3-8

Thanksgiving as we know it is a distinctly American holiday. Although a handful of other countries have Thanksgiving holidays, none are celebrated in the same manner or for the same reasons as in America.

Our Thanksgiving is a grand feast, accompanied by the camaraderie of friends and family—and a little football on the side. Schools shut down, people often travel halfway across the country, and we all finish the day stuffed to the gills.

All in the name of Thanksgiving.

Colossians 1:3-8 is our Thanksgiving meal. The turkey is there, together with the mouthwatering side dishes, down to the dessert that we can barely resist.

Even our game of football is available for us to enjoy.

Let's see how this passage stacks up next to our treasured American holiday.

First, we come with a thankful heart.

Thanksgiving is exactly what it says. We come to give thanks for all that we have received in life. We have breath in our lungs, food for our tongues, and companionship for our lonely hours.

Paul gives thanks for exactly the same things, for it is with the breath of God that life is breathed into us; he is our eternal source of sustenance; and it is in the cross that we find our companionship in him.

Paul writes with appreciation for all that

God has done for this body of believers, and he wants them to know his feelings. He desires them to know they are loved.

Second, we partake of food prepared by another's loving hand.

The Thanksgiving meal gives its greatest pleasure to the one whose hand has not prepared the table. Rather, it is in the savory aromas, and the beautifully set table, that we find our joy in the meal. If our hands do the preparation, sometimes all we can see is the work involved, and we miss the beauty that the meal has become.

Paul did not found the church at Colosse. Rather, it was founded by Epaphras. That gave Paul a unique perspective toward the Colossians. He was able to see the beauty of the meal, rather than the backbreaking work that had gone into its preparation. He states, "I have heard of your faith . . . and the love which you have for all the saints."

Paul takes special pleasure in this body of believers, because he sees them as they really are: a savory aroma rising before God Almighty.

Third, we anticipate the dessert that is to come.

At a Thanksgiving feast, desserts abound. They draw our attention as moths to a flame, even as the turkey arrives on its gleaming platter. Although we are not yet allowed to indulge these most tempting treats, nothing can expunge them from our thoughts.

Paul glories in the feast that is the church at Colosse. Yet, he also anticipates dessert. He knows there is a hope laid up for them in heaven. They have expressed faith in Christ, shown love to those who are like believers, and now can grasp the hope that is to come.

Paul even tells them where the dessert table is located. It is to be found "in the Word of the Truth of the Gospel."

Fourth, we enjoy the company of family and friends.

Without the company of our family and friends, Thanksgiving is nothing more than another plate of food to fill our stomachs for a time. Thanksgiving is what it is because of memories renewed, bonds that are strengthened, and love that grows in our hearts.

Paul recognized that in his letter to the Colossians. The message of the Christ that had come to them through Epaphras now connected this group of believers to the rest of the world, for they shared in the truth of the Christ, and their faith would continue to bring forth fruit, as it had already done.

Paul knew what many had yet to learn. God's grace only operates in the presence of truth. The church at Colosse had learned this lesson early, and it now strengthened them, fostering love in their hearts.

Fifth, we gather for the game, expecting our favored team to be victorious.

Football is a vicarious affair. There are few people who can sit to a Thanksgiving meal, and on the same day, rise to battle on the gridiron. Rather, we prefer to loosen our belts and let the pros have at it. In addition, it saves our muscles, keeping the bruises and abrasions of the game underneath someone else's jersey.

Paul praises a faithful companion of the gospel, one the believers at Colosse held in high esteem. He marches Epaphras onto the field in his pads and helmet, a victor in the Game of Salvation. He is the Colossians' hero, their champion on the field, for he is the one who brought the message of the Christ to Colosse.

Our Christianity is not vicarious, but to associate with one who has achieved success in the Lord builds us up, also.

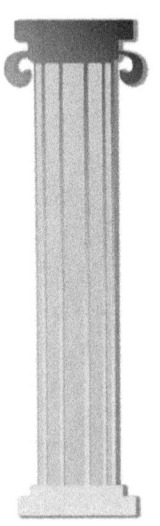

Sixth, we cheer for the victor, claiming his triumph as our own.

The television is on, and the game comes to a head. In the final moments of the final quarter, men leap to their feet, cheering the victor on the screen. There is no embarrassment, nor is there any hesitation in making our enthusiasm known. We want everyone to be aware that we chose the winning side.

Paul knew he was on the winning side, and he championed those who fought his same fight. He raises Epaphras high, for as he champions Epaphras before the body at Colosse, so has Epaphras championed the body before Paul.

It is the love produced by the Spirit of God that makes the victory possible. Paul recognizes that, and when we have our eyes opened, we will also know that there is only one way to become the victor. It is to fight with the Love of Christ as our banner and our sword.

In summary, when we come to God with a thankful heart, we will leave stuffed, for the victory he promises us will be ours.

Amen.

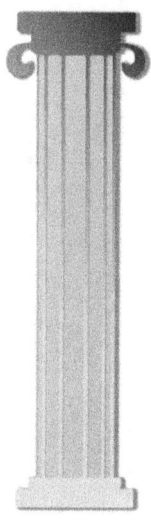

Read about it in the Bible:

Colossians 1:3-8 (KJV)

We give thanks to God and the Father of our Lord Jesus Christ, praying always for you, since we heard of your faith in Christ Jesus, and of the love which ye have to all the saints, for the hope which is laid up for you in heaven, whereof ye heard before in the word of the truth of the gospel; which is come unto you, as it is in all the world; and bringeth forth fruit, as it doth also in you, since the day ye heard of it, and knew the grace of God in truth: As ye also learned of Epaphras our dear fellowservant, who is for you a faithful minister of Christ; who also declared unto us your love in the Spirit.

A Thanksgiving Feast

Questions for Group Discussion

1. What message is the meat of the Bible? The obvious answer is probably correct.

2. If you pictured a part of the gospel as a dessert, what would it be?

3. If our walk with Jesus were a football game, who in your body would be the quarterback?

4. List three practical ways to cheer on those who serve the most demanding roles in your church body.

_____

_____

_____

5. Your church is having a Super Bowl party. Name three friends outside the church you could invite to attend.

_____

_____

_____

Brain Freeze

Colossians 1:9

Think of ice cream, cold soda, and coke floats. We dig in, chug them down, and leave the smiling residue on our faces.

What do we get in return? A brain freeze.

Brain freezes are very real.

What causes them? It is our body trying to warm the roof of our mouth. The blood vessels dilate, triggering pain receptors, and in the body's confusion, we feel the pain in our forehead.

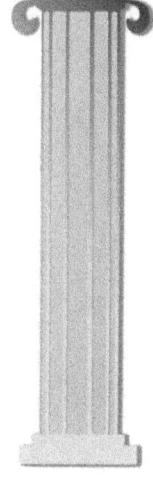

Brain freeze. It only lasts half a minute or so, and for most people, it is an exhilarating experience associated with the food we're eating. When we fill up on ice cream, our brain freeze is half the fun.

How do we get a brain freeze from God?

The same way. In fact, Paul encourages us to strive for a brain freeze, to consume so much of God that we hurt with exhilarating pain at the awesomeness of the Father.

In Colossians 1:9 we read how we can experience Paul's brain freeze. We simply dig in; chug it down; and smile in exhilaration.

Brain Freeze Step #1: Dig in.

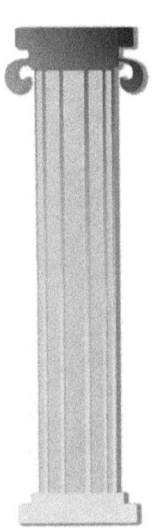

Paul encourages us to break out the ice cream. He knew how much the church at Colosse needed his spiritual support, and he wanted them filled with the knowledge of Christ.

Brain Freeze Step #2: Chug It Down.

Paul wants us to eat up as quickly as we can. When we consume as much of God as we can force inside, we will churn with excitement at his presence.

Brain Freeze Step #3: Smile in Exhilaration.

Paul knows the outcome of filling up on the Lord. We will receive wisdom and spiritual understanding, and we will have the same joy Paul experienced when he first came to the Lord. We will receive a brain freeze.

We can all experience a spiritual brain freeze. When we find truth and consume it as rapidly as possible, the reality of God in our lives will cause our bodies to react, triggering receptors that we didn't know were there. We will be supercharged for him, and we will look forward to filling up on God over and over, because we know the exhilaration of spending time with him.

In summary, when we fill up on God, he will affect us in a profound way.

Amen.

Read about it in the Bible:

Colossians 1:9 (KJV)

For this cause we also, since the day we heard it, do not cease to pray for you, and to desire that ye might be filled with the knowledge of his will in all wisdom and spiritual understanding;

Brain Freeze

Questions for Group Discussion

1. Write the names of three frozen treats people enjoy.

   _____

   _____

   _____

2. What is a verse that gives you chill bumps every time you read it?

   _____

   _____

   _____

3. Paul says to be "filled with the knowledge" of Christ. How can we do this?

   _____

   _____

   _____

4. List three times during the day you could plan five minutes to read the Word of God.

   _____

   _____

   _____

5. Who are three people you could text or email on a regular basis, telling them what you read that day in the Scriptures?

   _____

   _____

   _____

No Lifeguard on Duty

Colossians 1:10-13

Deep sea diving is one of the most hazardous jobs a person can undertake. To illustrate the risks divers take, hour for hour, it is 96 times more dangerous than driving a car.

What makes diving so dangerous?

Danger #1: Drowning.

This is the obvious one. Anyone who goes underwater faces this possibility. However, with a face mask, good swimming skills, and properly maintained equipment, it's not going to happen.

Danger #2: Pressure Changes.

Any number of consequences can develop from this: vertigo; burst eardrum; eye damage; lung damage. It is the proper equipment that will alleviate these concerns.

Danger #3: Gas Mixtures.

Decompression sickness is a killer, as is nitrogen narcosis or oxygen toxicity. Knowing the correct gas mixtures, or the appropriate rates of ascent, wipes these concerns from the slate.

Danger #4: The Diving Environment.

There is too much to list here. Hypothermia; hard corals; jellyfish; venomous spines; sharks; underwater hazards such as nets or cables. None of these can be accurately predicted, and all must be carefully assessed with each dive.

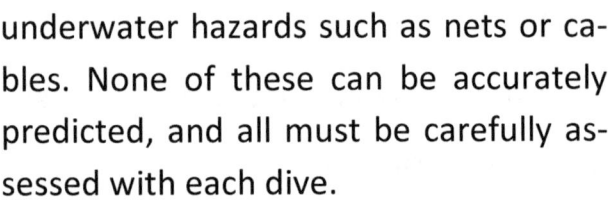

Yet, for those who dive, there is no greater thrill than to don scuba gear and take that plunge.

They leave the lifeguards on the beach, for they see the risks as minimal. After all, they know the precautions, and they are fully prepared in every way.

Our Christian walk is the same. We leap into each day with danger all around us.

Yet, in Colossians 1:10-13, Paul describes the layers of protection God's grace gives us in order to survive the perils of the world.

Grace Protection Layer #1: We are given a measure of grace that we might be worthy of the Lord, fully pleasing unto him.

It is through his wisdom and spiritual understanding that we become pleasing unto God, for the knowledge of the Lord proceeds from the inspiration of the Holy Spirit, alone.

Grace Protection Layer #2: We are fruitful in every good work.

We are to bear the fruit of the Father. It is our faith in the cross that brings about our good fruit. If we give the Holy Spirit the freedom to perfect our walk in the Lord, our good fruit is guaranteed.

Grace Protection Layer #3: We are increasing in the knowledge of God.

Our knowledge of God is based on our understanding of the cross. The Old Testament was the precursor. The revelation of the cross is the culmination. It is the finished work of Christ come to offer us salvation that is our true understanding.

Grace Protection Layer #4: We are strengthened with God's might.

Our strength comes according to God's glorious power. What are the signs we have received the strength of the Lord? We will show patience in all things, and we will be joyful in our long-suffering. Why suffer with joy? Because joy, through faith, guarantees victory.

Grace Protection Layer #5: We are partakers of the inheritance of the saints.

The believer in Christ becomes qualified to receive the inheritance of the saints by giving thanks unto the Father. That is all he wants from us, our hearts, offered to him in the praise and thanks we elevate before him.

Grace Protection Layer #6: We are translated into the kingdom of the Son.

Darkness is inherent in this world. However, Jesus has delivered us from that darkness, making us conquerors by the power of the cross. We recognize that the cross is not our end; rather it is the means by which we reach our end, which is the kingdom of heaven.

Deep sea diving is dangerous for the unprepared. However, when we are properly equipped and understand how to use what we've been given, the danger truly becomes of no consequence.

Our walk with God is the same. He prepares us with his grace, and when we understand how to use it, we will find our Christian walk a thrilling experience into the wonders of God's kingdom.

In summary, Jesus equips us for success, and when we wear his grace, lifeguards are no longer necessary. His grace is sufficient for our protection.

Amen.

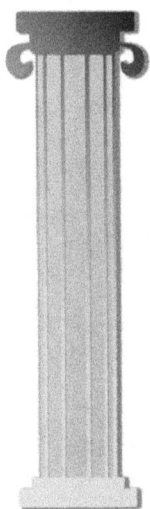

Read about it in the Bible:

Colossians 1:10-13 (KJV)

That ye might walk worthy of the Lord unto all pleasing, being fruitful in every good work, and increasing in the knowledge of God; Strengthened with all might, according to his glorious power, unto all patience and longsuffering with joyfulness; Giving thanks unto the Father, which hath made us meet to be partakers of the inheritance of the saints in light: Who hath delivered us from the power of darkness, and hath translated us into the kingdom of his dear Son:

No Lifeguard on Duty

Questions for Group Discussion

1. Describe a dangerous activity that you do, even if you do not consider it dangerous.

   _____

   _____

   _____

2. What safety measures do you use?

   _____

   _____

   _____

3. Have you ever taken a risk in your Christian walk? If so, what was it? If not, what held you back?

   _____

   _____

   _____

4. What is a time you were convinced the Hand of God kept you safe? (physically, spiritually, or emotionally)

_____

_____

_____

5. List three ways a Christian can equip himself for the dangers of the world.

_____

_____

_____

Trading Stamp Redemption

Colossians 1:14-15

In the year 1896 Thomas Sperry and Shelley Byron Hutchinson founded the Sperry and Hutchinson Company. To encourage sales they began issuing trading stamps that could be redeemed for free merchandise.

S&H Green Stamps weren't the only ones out there. Depending on where people lived, they might collect Triple S Stamps, Plaid Stamps, Top Value Stamps, or a number of others.

Each dollar spent earned a certain number of points, or stamps. They were often pasted in booklets and kept by the customer until they were ready for redemption. It could take years, one stamp at a time, to purchase something really big, like a refrigerator or a stove, or even a trip to Disneyland.

One stamp at a time.

Trading stamps are mostly discontinued now, converted to a digital version called reward points. However, leftover paper S&H Green Stamps are still valid and can be exchanged for the digital version simply by going online. Once given, they do not expire.

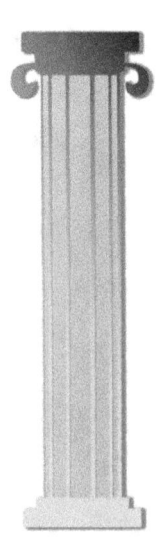

Jesus was the ultimate collector of trading stamps. He paid for them one at a time with each drop of blood he shed on the cross. **He even pasted them into a trading stamp booklet for us,** ready for us to take to the redemption center.

Our trading stamp booklet is called the Bible, and the stamps are the words that we read.

With our redemption book, we can purchase the biggest prize of all.

Eternal life.

Colossians 1:14-15 gives us the doctrine that we base our Christian faith on, but it gives us so much more. This passage is our trading stamp catalogue, telling us both the price and the prize available to us.

Each drop of Jesus' blood buys a stamp.

His shed blood adds up to a full booklet. Inside that booklet are enough stamps to provide us complete forgiveness of our sins. This passage even describes the product, for the Son whom we strive to emulate is the exact image of God the Father, the Creator of all things.

And we get it all for free.

Jesus holds it out to us, telling us to check the catalogue. There is a gift inside, he informs us, one that is so magnificent that no amount of money can purchase it. It is part of his redemption program, and his are the only trading stamps that can purchase it.

Trading stamp redemption, offered to us for free.

How great is that?

In summary, **Jesus paid the price so that we could have the gift of eternal life.** How can we refuse?

Amen.

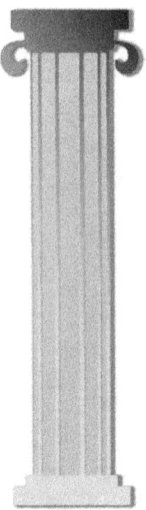

Read about it in the Bible:

Colossians 1:14-15 (KJV)

In whom we have redemption through his blood, even the forgiveness of sins: Who is the image of the invisible God, the firstborn of every creature:

Trading Stamp Redemption

Questions for Group Discussion

1. Have you ever gotten something for free, something besides a birthday or Christmas gift? If so, what was it?

   _____

   _____

2. Name something you have saved up to trade for an item. (boxtops, stamps, or even cash) What did you want to exchange it for?

   _____

   _____

3. Have you ever saved up so you could purchase someone else an item? If so, who was it for?

   _____

   _____

   _____

4. Which feels better, to gift our prize to ourselves, or to someone else? Why do you think that?

　_____

　_____

　_____

5. Jesus did not want to die on the cross. He pleaded for the Father to take that cup from him.

   Tell about a time someone gave up something important to them to give you a gift for free.

　_____

　_____

　_____

God's Glass Menagerie

Colossians 1:16

Some scientists argue that glass is really a fluid, although one that flows very slowly at ambient temperatures. They substantiate their claim by taking the measurements of millennia-old cathedral stained-glass windows; after a thousand years, the glass has become thinner at the top and thicker at the bottom.

It is simply a matter of temperature and state. **Apply sufficient heat, and the glass fully changes its state, becoming truly fluid, flowing easily into one shape or another.**

Watch a lamp-worker (otherwise known as a glass artist) work, and we see fanciful shapes come out of those little globs of molten sand. Plump penguins pirouette with panache, tiny tree houses tremble in the slightest breeze, and unbelievably intricate sailboats spin their glittering shards of light across the room. The glass artist is surrounded by a menagerie of his own creation, all as different as the artist's imagination, yet all the same in their beauty and mode of construction.

There is one indisputable fact in all this. Each item of fragile beauty had to become malleable in the glass artist's hands before it could become a thing of beauty.

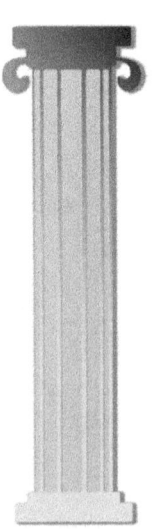

Colossians 1:16 tells us all the things we might find glittering in God's glorious menagerie. After all, his menagerie is all around us every day, filling the showcases of the heavens and the earth. Everything he has created surrounds us, if only we choose to open our eyes and see.

Let's open the showcases in God's Menagerie.

Showcase 1: The Glories of the Heavens

From the stars glittering in the night sky to the sun that warms our days, the heavens are nothing more than a trinket twisted out of nothing by the hand of the master glass artist. When we see a shooting star, a distant comet, or the soft glow of the Milky Way, we know we are in the midst of a vast menagerie of unimaginable proportions, all formed by the hand of God.

Showcase 2: The Things Under Our Feet

The ground is alive, from the earth's nickel core to the geysers of Yellowstone National Park. Poke the earth, and out erupts oil and gas. The continents shift, and earthquakes bellow the name of God our Father. The substance of our world glitters with God's beauty and power.

Showcase 3: All Things Visible

Those things that surround us are the visible discovery of our invisible God. We are created in his image, glass heated to a liquid state and re-shaped in the form of our Creator, duplicates down to our very nature. When we view the things that exist in the world around us, we take in the beautiful visage of our God.

Showcase 4: All Things Invisible

Some speak of the souls of man, invisible, as incomprehensible. However, they accept radio waves, magnetism, and gravity with aplomb. God has formed all things, even those we cannot see, with an artist's touch, to glorify the very existence of his presence. These are the things that exemplify the magnificence of our invisible God.

Showcase 5: Every Mighty Throne

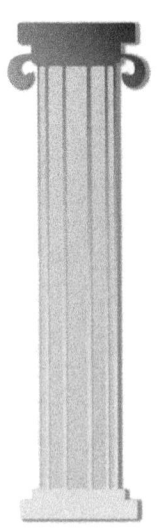

The thrones of the kingdom of man clearly fall into the realm of the visible, but the right to rule is an invisible one. Also consider the angels, for in ancient Jewish writings, they are said to sit upon thrones of power, created by the hand of God. The governments of this world are also God's to rule, for he has created each and every one. Whether kingdoms, angelic seats of power, or modern day governments, they are no more than baubles that glitter in the menagerie that belongs to the Father.

Showcase 6: Dominions, Principalities, and All the Powers that Be

There were those who wished to argue about who had the most power in heaven; false teachers taught that there were greater and lesser angels, often dividing the body of Christ with dissension and bickering. Paul skirted the entire issue, making it clear that God was the artist, and all things in God's creation, by any name, whether dominions, principalities, or powers, were no more than glittering trinkets in God's celestial showcase.

When we hold up a glass figurine from a lamp-worker's shop, it seems to sparkle with the fire of the sun, and in that fire, we imagine it to contain life.

It does, but it is life given by the hands of the artist, and without the artist, it is no more than a lump of sand.

In summary, God gives all life, for all things are created by his mighty hand.

There is no life without his divine will.

Amen.

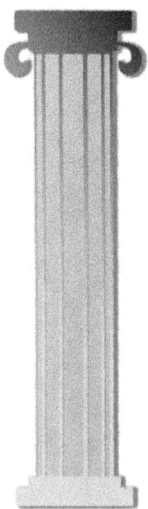

Read about it in the Bible:

Colossians 1:16 (KJV)

For by him were all things created, that are in heaven, and that are in earth, visible and invisible, whether they be thrones, or dominions, or principalities, or powers: all things were created by him, and for him:

God's Glass Menagerie

Questions for Group Discussion

1. List three things you have on display in your home.

   _____

   _____

   _____

2. Describe something you made on your own, from a greeting card to a piece of furniture. Did you keep it or give it away?

   _____

   _____

   _____

3. What is a subject you know so well you could give a talk about it? What three facts or concepts would you include in your talk?

   _____

   _____

4. Paul was a tentmaker. He knew how to sew sailcloth. What is a skill you could donate to your local church?

_____

_____

_____

5. God wants us to "sparkle with the fire of the sun." In your walk with him, how have people seen that fire in you? If they haven't, what can you change to ensure that they do?

_____

_____

_____

Jesus in Focus

Colossians 1:17-19

Ask a young girl to describe her father, and her description of who he is to her will be seen through the lens of love. She may tell of the thickness of his hair, or the strength of his arms. Her words may describe how he smells when he hugs her or the sound of his laugh when he is amused.

One thing will always be the same, though. She will tell how he is, not how he's changed, who he once was, or who he will someday be.

Her lens is focused on the present, for

to her, he is not a high school football star or a starry-eyed romantic wooing her mother. He is not a retiree golfing his days away. He is simply her father. He is the way he is, he has always been that way, and he will be the same forever. That's what she sees through her lens. That's her father in focus.

Describing Jesus is pretty much the same. We must focus on who he is, and when we see his person and his nature clearly, we will better know the one we love.

Paul in Colossians 1:17-19 gives us a pretty clear description of who Jesus is in six focused statements.

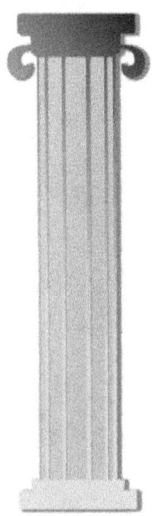

Statement #1: Jesus existed before all things were created.

The divine nature of the Christ didn't suddenly materialize in that manger so many centuries ago. Rather, as Jesus said in John 8:58, he existed before the coming of man. Jesus is part of the very plan of our world, here before it was created, and part of that creation itself.

Statement #2: Jesus created all things.

As Jesus was here before our world was created, so it was his hand that helped sculpt the mountains and valleys, reaching down to scoop out the basins of the seas. He participated in forming man from the dust of the ground and breathing life into his lungs. All things in existence reflect the nature of his personality, for that which he has created is part of who he is.

Statement #3: Jesus is the head of the church.

Christ must be the center of the church's beliefs. To say Jesus is the head of the church is to say he is a definitive part of the church, firmly attached, and vital to the functioning of the church. He loves the church and cares for her as his own flesh, for indeed the church is the body of Jesus. The two cannot be separated.

Statement #4: Jesus is the originator of the church.

The Jewish faith had become rote, and in its failure to meet the spiritual needs of the people, a new covenant was made between God and humanity. The church as we know it today started with the seed of Jesus, planted in Golgotha's soil, and raised to life in a rocky tomb carved into the hillside. If any other comes to us with a new way to heaven, there is no truth in his spoken words. Jesus is the New Covenant, and in him and him alone does our salvation rest.

Statement #5: Jesus is the firstborn from the dead.

Not only is Jesus the head and originator of the church, he is the first to be born of humanity's flesh and resurrected into the immortality of our blessed hope. He is our example and our promise that one day we will also be resurrected into our heavenly bodies to join with him in worship of the Father.

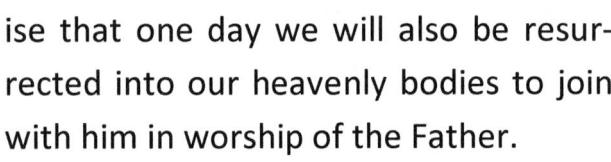

Statement #6: Jesus is the supreme authority in all things.

Jesus is the firstborn of the Father; the firstborn of all creation; the only begotten Son of the Father. Just as in our human families, being firstborn gives not only special privileges, but also special responsibilities. More is required of a firstborn child than of a younger sibling.

As the firstborn of the Father, Jesus was required to become our redemption, and in the same manner, he was given the privilege to become our salvation, the one to whom we draw for the forgiveness of our sins.

Paul wraps up this passage with the statement, "For it pleased the Father that in him should all fullness dwell."

Just as that little girl is filled with pride when she describes her father, so our Heavenly Father is pleased with Jesus.

He is so pleased that he has given unto his Son the complete and total power of the Godhead.

All the power of the heavenly realm is Jesus' to dispense, and when he becomes our head, and we become his body, there is no limit to what he will do for and through us.

In summary, when we focus on the nature of Jesus, we begin to understand why he loves us so much.

Amen.

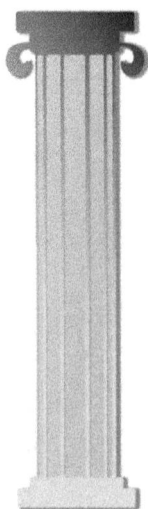

Read about it in the Bible:

Colossians 1:17-19 (KJV)

And he is before all things, and by him all things consist. And he is the head of the body, the church: who is the beginning, the firstborn from the dead; that in all things he might have the preeminence. For it pleased the Father that in him should all fullness dwell;

Jesus in Focus

Questions for Group Discussion

1. What did you excel at in high school? Don't be modest; be sure to take this opportunity to brag on yourself.

　

　

　

2. Tell about something one of your parents is (or was) especially good at. What makes that stand out to you?

　

　

　

3. What would you like your children (or other relatives) to see you as? List several things.

4. How do you see Jesus? Use words of your own, not just "churchy" words.

_____

_____

_____

5. What are some things we can do to change the world's view of Jesus?

_____

_____

_____

Simon Says

Colossians 1:20-22

We've all played that playground game. Simon says, Jump! And we all jump.

And keep jumping until Simon says, Stop!

At first glance it seems as though the game is a dictatorship, one where the caller has all the power.

Everyone must obey the commands given or be eliminated by attrition, one player at a time.

The caller can even trip up the players

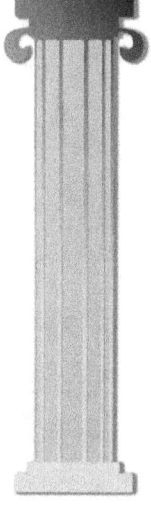

by issuing a command without prefacing it with the words, "Simon says." To follow an incorrectly stated command is to be kicked out just as surely as if not following a command at all.

Yet, this game has a vastly different connotation in the life of the Christian.

Rather than seeing it as a dictatorship, we must look at the game as one of unity, one where each member follows the rules set up by the player acting as Simon. If one player reaches to tie her shoes, and another scratches his head, the game collapses in anarchy.

Only when the players work as a team does the game function as intended.

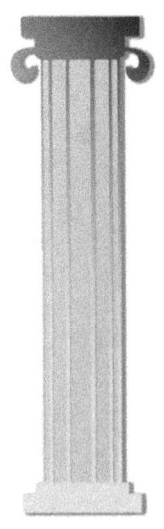

In Colossians 1:20-22, Christ is our Simon. He brings players from all walks of life together to bind them in unity. From the rough dockworker telling coarse jokes to the financial advisor debating whether she can get away with skimming funds from her accounts, Christ draws them to himself, setting a standard prefaced by the phrase, Simon says.

The game is a simple one, and easy to play. All we have to do is listen and follow along. Let's see how it is done:

Simon says:

> **Peace comes through my blood shed on the cross.**

The rules of the game have to be established. Jesus (Simon) tells us the rules before he begins to play. We must be together on this, for to play any other way is to collapse into anarchy. The basis for our Christian walk is to believe that we come to him through his blood, and there is no other way.

Simon says:

> **Through your faith, I will reconcile all things unto me.**

We have to be able to trust his commands. If Jesus asks us to tie our shoelaces, we must immediately drop to our knees and begin tying our shoelaces. We must have faith in

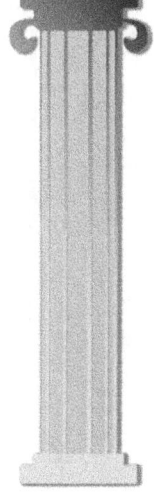

what he asks us to do, or we cannot follow him.

Simon says:

All things in heaven and in earth are under my command.

Only one person can be the caller. Jesus. In this statement, he makes it clear that the individual players cannot call the shots. If Jesus says to tie our shoes, and we choose to scratch our heads, then we have abrogated his authority, and there will be no unity within the body of Christ.

Simon says:

You were alienated, yet I chose you to become one with me.

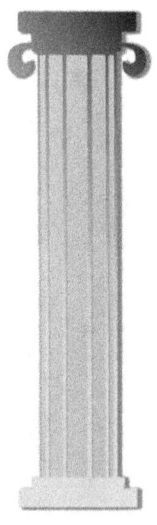

We do not play this game through lack of choice. There are other games on the playground: greed; lust; anger; overindulgence; laziness; jealously; pride. These are the games that come naturally to humanity. They are also the games that alienate us from the Savior. Yet, Christ says, although you are human, I want you to play my game, one of purity, self-restraint, generosity, and humility.

Simon says:

I came from heaven to become human, and I died for you.

These are Christ's qualifications to play the part of Simon. The Christ, one-third of the Godhead, a portion of the triumvirate that created all that was, is, and is to come, chose to relinquish his seat at the right hand of the Father that he might know what it is to be truly human. Then, he allowed himself to be crucified on the cross that his death might provide atonement for our humanity.

Simon says:

I lift you as unified and without flaw before my Father in heaven.

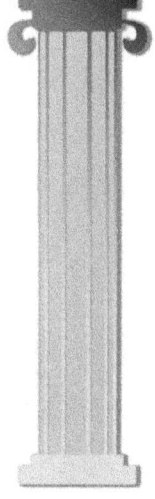

This is our gift when we choose to abandon all the other games on the playground and play with the Christ. When we choose the game of Simon Says, we choose to play with Christ as our Simon, and we also choose unity with the almighty God in the heavens.

When Christ says, "Simon says," he isn't playing dictator.

Rather, he is drawing us out of the world and into the purity and humility that God demands. When we choose to follow his commands, we will become like him in all things, and we will know heaven as our eternal home.

In summary, when we follow Jesus' commands, he will brag to the Father about us.

Amen.

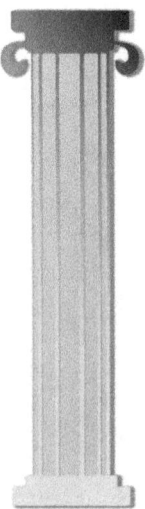

Read about it in the Bible:

Colossians 1:20-22 (KJV)

And, having made peace through the blood of his cross, by him to reconcile all things unto himself; by him, I say, whether they be things in earth, or things in heaven. And you, that were sometime alienated and enemies in your mind by wicked works, yet now hath he reconciled in the body of his flesh through death, to present you holy and unblameable and unreproveable in his sight:

Simon Says

Questions for Group Discussion

1. Who are some people you associate with in the church that you might never have met otherwise?

   _____

   _____

   _____

2. Jesus' disciples came from varying walks of life. Research out three disciples and list their professions.

   _____

   _____

   _____

3. Write three things you can do personally to achieve unity rather than a dictatorship in your family.

   _____

   _____

4. Just as Jesus did, a number of early Christians gave their lives for what they believed. Name several, and if you know, tell how they died.

   _____

   _____

   _____

5. Research the name of a missionary who died on the mission field. How did his or her death promote the gospel of Christ?

   _____

   _____

   _____

The Wall of Honor

Colossians 1:23-29

The Vietnam Veterans Memorial is a stunning testimony to the 58,000 soldiers who lost their lives during the Vietnam era in a war that wasn't really a war. Erected in 1982, not only does the ebony surface list the names of those who died, it also reflects back the faces of those still living.

The Vietnam Veterans Memorial is a bridge between the living and the dead, entangling those who gave their lives with the people they died for. It also testifies to the pedigree of each of the men and women listed on its face. They are soldiers and heroes, one and all, for they gave the ultimate sacrifice for their country.

The Vietnam Veterans Memorial is a Wall of Honor, meant to show our nation's pride in her most precious sons and daughters. The memorial also substantiates individual soldier's lives, telling the proof that they are due the honor they are given.

In Colossians 1:23-29 Paul felt the need to erect a Wall of Honor.

He needed to erect a bridge between the living and the dead, to reflect the faces of the living in the accounts of the dead, and to entangle the one who gave his life on the cross with the people he died for.

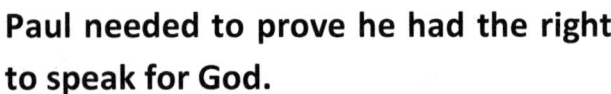

Paul needed to prove he had the right to speak for God.

So, Paul raised his memorial high, penning his words to the believers at Colosse, one of three cities grouped in the Lycus Valley. The local church, originally founded by a man named Epaphras, was now being misled by men teaching false doctrine. Paul had to offer proof that he had the qualifications and the right to straighten them out.

Paul did it with a Wall of Honor. What did Paul list on his Wall of Honor? His sacrifices and qualifications. Let's look at the proof Paul offered:

Proof #1: I have been made a minister of the faith brought to you by Epaphras.

> Paul connected himself to the church at Colosse. Just as they had heard the message of the Christ, so that same hope formed the core of Paul's ministry.

Proof #2: I am suffering for you, so that Christ's suffering may be complete.

> Paul was in prison as he wrote this letter. Yet, he considered himself lucky to be worthy of suffering for Jesus. He felt it was the least he could do for his Lord, who had suffered even unto death.

Proof #3: God wishes me to bring to you, the gentiles, a new message of

hope.

Paul had received the New Covenant. He refused to become embroiled in any discussion that did not center on the message of the cross. It was the only message that counted.

Proof #4: I bring to you, Christ's saints, the great secret of the ages, unfolded and offered to you for your sanctification.

Up to this time, the gospel had been reserved for the Jews. Now, it was offered to the gentiles, manifested to the believers, including those at Colosse, who would now be full partakers of the New Covenant made flesh by the cross.

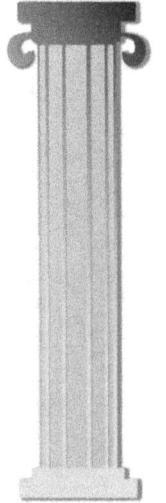

Proof #5: As Christ lives in me, so Christ in you is your only hope of glory.

Paul was not a salesman, hoping to ameliorate deteriorating conditions in Colosse by a Band-Aid approach. Rather, the solution he offered was one that lived in him, one that minded no racial or political barriers, and one that was made possible by the cross. He offered Jesus.

Proof #6: I endeavor to bring all men to Christ, that I may present them to God, perfect in every way through Jesus Christ.

> Paul knew of the false teachings in Colosse. He wished the believers there to mature in truth and wisdom, for only then could they stand perfect before God. Paul also felt the onus on his shoulders, for God had given him the responsibility to share the gospel with all men.

Proof #7: I can do this through the power of the Christ who lives in me.

> Paul acknowledges his own human frailty. He never lost sight of the change Christ made in him, taking him from persecutor of the church to purveyor of the New Covenant. He boasts in the cross as his strength and strong bulwark.

Those of us who have visited the Vietnam Veterans Memorial have seen ourselves overlaid on the names written with such honor on that black stone. Now we look at Paul's Wall of Honor. Our faces are reflected in his words. Do we dare ask how we compare?

In summary, even if we close our eyes, the world continues to see us as we are. Let's make sure it is the honor of Christ that is reflected in our actions.

Amen.

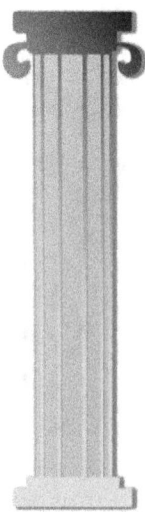

Read about it in the Bible:

Colossians 1:23-29 (KJV)

If ye continue in the faith grounded and settled, and be not moved away from the hope of the gospel, which ye have heard, and which was preached to every creature which is under heaven; whereof I Paul am made a minister; Who now rejoice in my sufferings for you, and fill up that which is behind of the afflictions of Christ in my flesh for his body's sake, which is the church: Whereof I am made a minister, according to the dispensation of God which is given to me for you, to fulfil the word of God; Even the mystery which hath been hid from ages and from generations, but now is made manifest to his saints: To whom God would make known what is the riches of the glory of this mystery among the Gentiles; which is Christ in you, the hope of glory: Whom we preach, warning every man, and teaching every man in all wisdom;

That we may present every man perfect in Christ Jesus: Whereunto I also labor, striving according to his working, which worketh in me mightily.

The Wall of Honor

Questions for Group Discussion

1. Name three military branches of the United States of America. (There are more than three!)

   _____

   _____

   _____

2. Name someone in your family who served in a war and was injured. What war was it? Do you view them differently knowing they were injured in a war?

   _____

   _____

3. What about someone in prison? Paul was in prison. How do you think his contemporaries felt about that?

   _____

   _____

4. Has anyone ever argued with you about the Scriptures? If so, what about? Did the disagreement get resolved?

   _____

   _____

   _____

5. Do you have a wall of honor in your house? If so, what is displayed there? (examples: photos, awards, memorabilia)

   _____

   _____

   _____

Blinded by Fog

Colossians 2:1-3

Fog is a fact of life for anyone who lives near the sea. Ships are especially vulnerable. When warm air evaporates water while over land, this moisture-laden air can be drawn over the water, condensing into water droplets around salt particles dispersed throughout the cooler sea air.

The ships become blinded by fog.

However, even though they cannot see, the ships still have a method of safe passage through the wall of blindness. They can pull out a VHF radio, as well as use a good set of ears, a compass, a radar reflector, a chart, and a horn.

The troubles of life often blind us to the truths of the spiritual world.

Confusion rolls in like fog across the sea. One moment we are sure we know just where we're going, and we feel we have everything under control. Then, a wall of fog hits us, and we are sailing blind.

The believers at Colosse were sailing blind. False teachers were leading them astray. Fog had them surrounded. Then a voice called to them in the guise of an epistle written by a man they'd never met, an apostle named Paul.

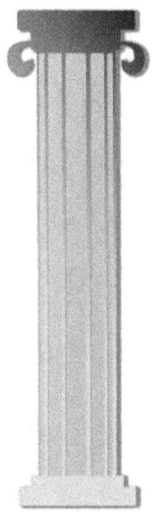

Paul didn't plant the church at Colosse. They didn't know him personally. However, Paul reached out to them through the fog that had engulfed them, and he offered them a way through the blindness.

Colossians 2:1-3 lists the tools God gives us to ensure our safe passage through the fog:

Tool #1: A VHF Radio

We cannot see the person at the other end of the radio. Yet, we have to depend on his qualifications and that he will not lead us astray. That voice coming over the radio reaches through the fog and guides us to the other side.

Paul says to the believers at Colosse, "You have not seen my face in the flesh."

However, he was their VHF radio, calling to them through the fog, giving them directions around their obstacles.

Tool #2: A Good Set of Ears

It is frightening to not be able to see where we are headed. Our daughter goes off to college, just as the stock market drops. We choose early retirement, only to find an unexpected lump beneath our skin. We take a chance on love, but the bubble bursts, and we are devastated.

Paul wishes that the hearts of those in Colosse might be comforted.

How? By listening to the truth that comes from the Father. In this case, that truth is found in Paul's missive to the Colossians, written from his cell in Rome.

Tool #3: A Compass

A good compass always points to true north. If the needle swings any other direction, and we follow its leading, we will become lost. A ship sailing in the fog cannot trust a compass that does not tell the true direction it needs to travel.

What is our compass in Christ? It is the love that ties the church together.

Paul affirms this, for he tells the Colossians to be knit together with one another in love. If they follow that love, they will never be lost, no matter what obscures their vision.

Tool #4: A Radar Reflector

When a ship is entombed in fog, other ships have to know where it is. Radar is blind if nothing reflects the signals back. As Christians, we must know the truth, so that when others see us, we can ensure that Christ is reflected back to them.

The believers at Colosse were being led astray. **Paul wished for them to have a full understanding of the cross, for only then could they have the assurance that their walk was pleasing to God.** Only then could they reflect Christ to the world.

Tool #5: A Chart

A nautical chart shows underwater obstacles that might sink our ship. When we know the obstacles that are in our way, we can better avoid the devastation.

Our chart is found in our understanding of the mystery of God, revealed by both the Father and the Christ.

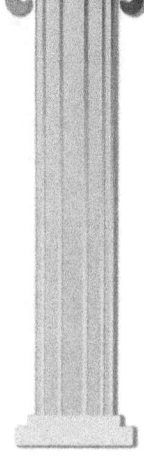

When we see the truths of the divine, the fog won't matter, because God has already ordered our steps. We only have to follow the paths he has charted.

Tool #6: A Horn

A ship sailing in fog announces its presence loudly and clearly. There must be no doubt it is there. For land-based foghorns, patterns reveal which horn is sounding using different pitches and frequency, telling where the horn is located.

Our horn is heard in our actions, love, and empathy for others.

When the treasures of wisdom and knowledge, hidden within our God, are revealed to us, we will shout our love to others, because we won't have any other choice.

The church at Colosse was sailing through the fog of false teachings. Paul knew they needed directions, or else they would run aground and founder. From his prison cell, he gave them the guidance they needed.

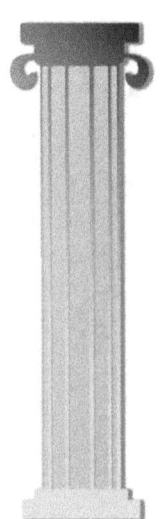

We can find our spiritual direction in Christ, no matter how thick the fog that obscures our view of the future.

When we listen to him, he will faithfully

guide us home.

In summary, **Jesus is never lost.** When we follow him, we will always survive the storm.

Amen.

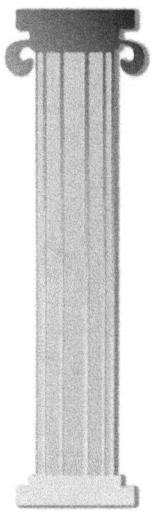

Read about it in the Bible:

Colossians 2:1-3 (KJV)

For I would that ye knew what great conflict I have for you, and for them at Laodicea, and for as many as have not seen my face in the flesh; That their hearts might be comforted, being knit together in love, and unto all riches of the full assurance of understanding, to the acknowledgement of the mystery of God, and of the Father, and of Christ; In whom are hid all the treasures of wisdom and knowledge.

Blinded by Fog

Questions for Group Discussion

1. Not all fog is literal. What can cause spiritual fog?

   _____

   _____

   _____

2. List three items that young people today have to wrestle with that didn't affect your generation.

   _____

   _____

   _____

3. What is your church's rallying cry? This is something you hear repeatedly that immediately triggers you to think of the body of Christ.

   _____

   _____

   _____

4. What makes your church strong? Give three reasons people should attend your congregation and not somewhere else.

   _____

   _____

   _____

5. If you moved into your city, would you choose your fellowship over again? How can you encourage others to attend your church?

   _____

   _____

   _____

Blowing Out the Candle

Colossians 2:4-10

During birthday parties, we encourage small children to blow out a candle and make a wish. Anything they want can be theirs, we say. Then, believe, or the wish won't come true. We do the same at Christmas and when losing a tooth. Ask for anything, because it just might come true.

When Solomon was given the chance to ask for anything he wanted, he didn't ask for a greater kingdom than his father or for an increase in the national treasury. He already had everything. Instead, he asked for something much simpler, something intangible, and something most people wouldn't think of.

Solomon asked for wisdom.

Sometimes modern Christians struggle with asking for the correct things from God. We believe on the Lord, Jesus Christ; we take pride in the charity we afford others; and we think we've done all we need to do. However, God wants us to be an example of his love. Paul told the believers at Corinth that even with their abundant charity and faith, without love, they had nothing. Love was the greatest of the three.

Even Jesus said we were to love God first, then love our neighbor as ourselves, for there was no greater command he could give.

It seems obvious that wisdom and love are the two treasures the Lord values above all else. Slide those two words together, and we get, quite literally, wisdom-love.

Wisdom-love. The love of wisdom. In one word, to be specific, philosophy.

If the literal definition of philosophy is the love of wisdom, then what is a practical definition? It is to look at the problems around us and try to understand them in connection with reality as we know it.

However, to do this, we have three concepts to consider:

Concept #1: Societal Values

This is another way of saying, our basic beliefs. What are our fables (telling our moral attitudes), and the behaviors we expect from those around us?

Concept #2: Reasonableness

Does what we suggest make sense in the world as we know it? Will our suggestions, or conclusions, be accepted by those around us? Can we take what we already know and make sense of it?

Concept #3: Attitudes of Individuals and the General Public

As the world changes around us, our level of knowledge constantly increases. How does that affect us, and how does that change who we are? How do we live with those changes and retain our humanity with respect to each other?

One man's definition of philosophy is to take facts that do not fit neatly into any of our convenient "solutions" and figure out how they work into our system of beliefs.

Jesus and the message of the cross was one of those facts that would not fit into society's system of beliefs. Paul addressed this in Colossians 2:4-10.

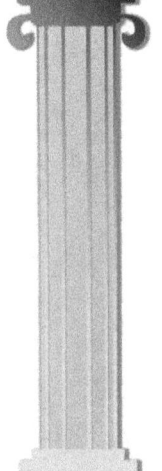

First, Paul tells us not to be deceived, no matter how persuasive someone's argument.

The church at Colosse was facing deceptive teachings. They were being taught that they could achieve the perfection of Christ through their own works. It seemed good to them, but it was leading them astray. They had to get back to the cross.

Second, he reassures us that we are one in Christ, linked through the Spirit of God.

Paul acknowledged that he was not physically with the believers at Colosse. Neither had he established the church at Colosse. Nor could he travel to visit with them. He was in prison at the time. Yet, he pointed out the link that bound them as one, the Holy Spirit, and he encouraged the believers to continue in the steadfastness of Christ.

Third, our goal is to stand on our salvation in Christ Jesus.

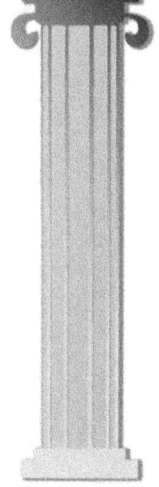

When we first come to Christ, our lives are all about Jesus. It is only later that other concerns wedge themselves in, and we begin to draw away. Paul encouraged the Colossians to remember that moment when they first found their faith. That was where they needed to return.

Fourth, society's traditions and the laws of nature cannot structure our walk with Christ.

Philosophy was being used to brush aside the mysteries of the cross, citing traditional beliefs and the natural laws of the physical world. However, Jesus is of the spiritual world, and the normal rules do not apply. If we believe otherwise, we let the devil cheat us out of our salvation.

Fifth, Jesus is one with the Father.

Some religions, even today, teach that Jesus was no more than a good man, a prophet who died upon the cross. However, Paul makes it clear that he is much more. Jesus has the fullness of the Godhead living in him.

Sixth, when we walk with Christ, we need no other guide.

We need only look to Jesus for our direction. When men come to us with teachings that do not include the cross, we must look away, searching until we have Jesus fully back in our sights.

Blow out a candle and make a wish. That is childhood fantasy. Rather, we should read the Word and follow Jesus. Philosophy helps us understand the world. The Bible helps us understand ourselves.

Once we understand what the Bible says, there is no question but that if we follow in the steps of Jesus, we will receive life everlasting. The Bible tells us so.

In summary, when we hear a message other than Jesus on the cross, we must return to the Word, for there we will find spiritual truth.

Amen.

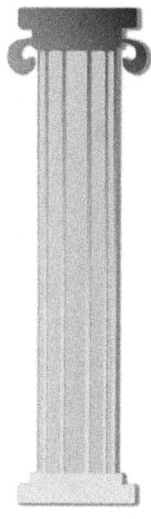

Read about it in the Bible:

Colossians 2:4-10 (KJV)

And this I say, lest any man should beguile you with enticing words. For though I be absent in the flesh, yet am I with you in the spirit, joying and beholding your order, and the steadfastness of your faith in Christ. As ye have therefore received Christ Jesus the Lord, so walk ye in him: Rooted and built up in him, and established in the faith, as ye have been taught, abounding therein with thanksgiving. Beware lest any man spoil you through philosophy and vain deceit, after the tradition of men, after the rudiments of the world, and not after Christ. For in him dwelleth all the fullness of the Godhead bodily. And ye are complete in him, which is the head of all principality and power:

Blowing Out the Candle

Questions for Group Discussion

1. In a nutshell, what is the message of the cross?

   _____

   _____

   _____

2. Write a simple version of the sinner's prayer.

   _____

   _____

   _____

3. Tell the story of when you first came to Christ. How did you respond emotionally?

   _____

   _____

   _____

4. How can you be an example to those you don't see day-to-day? List three ways.

    _____

    _____

    _____

5. Write your response to these three statements:

    Man can achieve perfection through good works.

    _____

    Jesus was a good man who died on the cross.

    _____

    Science has all the answers we need.

    _____

1-800-GOJESUS

Colossians 2:11-23

We all know the lawyer jokes. We hear them all the time. From the one with three lawyers in a sinking ship, to God teeing off against a dead lawyer in heaven, they always have a punch line that puts the lawyer on an equal footing with sharks.

However, our legal system, cumbersome as it is, is what maintains the basis of our society. Someone slander us? There are laws for clearing our name. Identity theft? We put 1-800-LAWYERS on our speed dial to begin the road to restitution.

Yet, laws can sometimes be tricky to navigate. Just look at the American tax code. The legal wrangling that keeps corporations on good terms with Uncle Sam can require a legal team hundreds of lawyers strong.

Laws dictate how we live our lives.

From gated neighborhoods where we are told what color to paint our garage doors to wetland protections that drown landowners in restrictive restoration, we dance to stay within the strict statutes that define our American way of life.

At the time of Christ, the religious world of the Jews was the same. Laws dictated the tricky trails that led to the pearly gates.

Wear this garment on this day; eat this food only at certain times; and be humble, even if false humility was considered better than no humility at all. The requirements were cumbersome, stealing people's identities, and the only recourse was to call 1-800-PRIESTS.

It was the temple hotline, and the only one available.

In Colossians 2:11-23, Paul gave the church at Colosse a better way.

Christ's way.

Mosaic Law, or "Temple Law," was well and good in its day. The children of Israel had lived four centuries under the dominion of their Egyptian overlords, and they needed a handbook for following God. However, they never got past using the handbook. They never learned the real lessons of how to incorporate the message of God into their lives, to make God so intrinsic to their very being that they wanted to live for him every day, rather than simply following the primer that God had given them centuries before.

Jesus was Mosaic Law, Volume 2.

What was the opening precept in Jesus' book? Jesus came to fulfill the law, and in doing so, he set the law aside. Why? The law was ineffectual in reaching its desired end. It had not created a spiritual nation. It had created a legalistic nation.

Jesus' presence on earth was about the spirit, not legalistic wrangling simply to keep the temple priests happy.

If, as Christians, we establish a set of rules that converts must follow, and the rules become more important than our relationship with Christ, then we have missed the mark. We will stand tall, and the world will applaud our success, and the angels in heaven will weep in despair over our delusions.

What did Paul tell the body at Colosse? **Legalism is not the path to salvation. Christ is.** Paul even listed those laws that the believers should cast aside as no more than legalistic burdens, laws designed for the time before Christ, but now put aside by Christ's death on the cross.

Legalistic Burden #1: Circumcision

In Genesis 17 God made a covenant with Abraham. Abraham was given a new start; brought from childlessness to a new birth; and given a new lease on life. Circumcision was to be a daily reminder of that covenant.

Yet, Paul says that Jesus nailed the requirements of circumcision to the cross.

Our new life is not a physical one. Rather, it is a spiritual one. Our old man was buried with Christ, and our new man arose with him from the dead, into triumph. Christ has cut away the dead flesh, and he is our covenant, residing with us every day.

Legalistic Burden #2: Food and Drink

Leviticus 11 gives a whole smorgasbord of food restrictions for the Jewish people. Pork; most seafood; insects; scavenger birds. Food sacrificed to idols was also a big issue in the 1st century church.

Part of the problem came from culture and heritage.

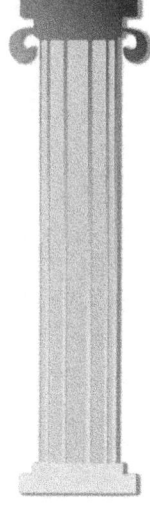

Those of Jewish background could not change embedded teachings in so short a time, and the gentiles were being pushed to follow suit. However, Paul made it clear that the principles of "Do not touch; do not taste; do not handle" no longer applied.

Legalistic Burden #3: Festivals and Sabbaths

Jewish culture was steeped in history. To remember who they were and why they worshipped one god, the Jews observed a litany of holidays and festivals: Purim; Passover; Shavuot; Rosh Hashanah; Yom Kippur; and more.

The cross and the redemption we receive is the finished work of Christ.

The observances of the Jewish faith were no more than a shadow of the Christ to come. When we have the real thing, why do we need shadows and dreams?

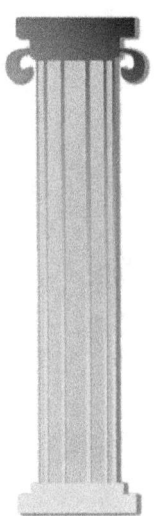

Legalistic Burden #4: False Humility

Public humiliation was often considered a penance for sin. Self-abasement, especially long and pious prayers, was one way of raising one's standing among those of the Jewish faith. However, when our prayers and self-abasement are for our own benefit, then they are of no benefit at all.

This was especially apropos to those in the Colossian body.

Teachers, bearing false humility and false doctrine, were pushing the teachings of Christ aside. Rather, Paul suggests, our humility must come from Christ, alone, and not from the desire to elevate ourselves before others.

Legalistic Burden #5: Worship of Angels

Gnostic teachings had begun to infiltrate the church at Colosse. This belief said that Jesus was not our direct line to God. Rather, there were layers of angel intermediaries that we must traverse first. Some even taught that Jesus attained divinity through works and taught his disciples to do the same.

The truth is that there is no way to God except through the cross.

If we attempt to find God through our own means, we will fail. We must trust in Jesus and his finished work on the cross.

Paul wraps up this passage, reminding

us that the regulations of this world may have an appearance of wisdom, but they will perish.

Whether we turn to self-imposed religion, false humility, or self-abasement, these things cannot bring us closer to God.

When Christ died, he arose a new man. When we die in Christ, the basic principles of the world no longer apply to us. We are new creatures in him, part of the body of Christ, and we only grow when we are planted in him.

In summary, when times get rough, our hotline is 1-800-GOJESUS. It is the only number we need to call.

Amen.

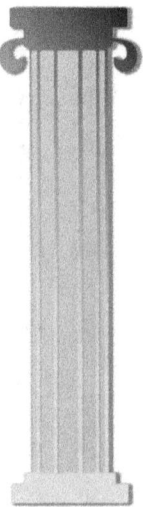

Read about it in the Bible:

Colossians 2:11-23 (KJV)

In whom also ye are circumcised with the circumcision made without hands, in putting off the body of the sins of the flesh by the circumcision of Christ: Buried with him in baptism, wherein also ye are risen with him through the faith of the operation of God, who hath raised him from the dead. And you, being dead in your sins and the uncircumcision of your flesh, hath he quickened together with him, having forgiven you all trespasses; Blotting out the handwriting of ordinances that was against us, which was contrary to us, and took it out of the way, nailing it to his cross; And having spoiled principalities and powers, he made a show of them openly, triumphing over them in it. Let no man therefore judge you in meat, or in drink, or in respect of an holy day, or of the new moon, or of the Sabbath days: Which are a shadow of things to come; but the body is of Christ. Let no man beguile you of your reward in a voluntary humility and worshipping of angels, intruding into those things which he hath not seen, vainly puffed up by his fleshly mind, and not holding the head, from which all the body by joints and bands having nourishment ministered, and knit together, increaseth with the increase of God. Wherefore if ye be dead with Christ from the rudiments of the world, why, as though living in the world, are ye subject to ordinances, (Touch not; taste not; handle not; Which all are to perish with the using;) after the commandments and doctrines of men? Which things have indeed a show of wisdom in will worship, and humility, and neglecting of the body: not in any honor to the satisfying of the flesh.

1-800-GOJESUS

Questions for Group Discussion

1. How can a law be beneficial to one person and detrimental to another?

   _____

   _____

   _____

2. Name a law (or rule) in your community that you think is unevenly enforced.

   _____

   _____

   _____

3. List some church "rules" that might be more tradition than scripture.

   _____

   _____

   _____

4. What was Jesus' number one law/rule? Think golden here.

   _____

   _____

   _____

5. How do the rules of the church, even those that derive from tradition, make the body stronger?

   _____

   _____

   _____

Planting October's Spring Garden

Colossians 3:1-4

We think of October as fall festival season, with pumpkins piled high, brightly colored leaves fluttering through the air, and scarves to keep our necks warm. We revel at the chill in the air.

The summer flowers have bloomed their last, and the flowerbeds are barren. Even the birds have headed south, their whistling melodies taken with them. Soon fresh snow will blanket the world, and we will hunker down until spring arrives.

However, there is still October's garden to prepare. Oh, this will not be a garden of winter's flowers with brightly colored blooms. October's garden will be there, patiently waiting, in order to offer us a spring delight. It is a labor of love that takes the whole winter to flower. We make a master plan, dig our holes, position next spring's bulbs, and mulch them carefully. Deep in that dark hole, unseen to us, they will put out roots, reaching long fingers into the soil, preparing to thrust through to the warmth of the sun once the snows have gone.

We are those bulbs, and life is our garden. We must be planted, so that when Christ comes, bringing us a new spring, we can burst forth victorious in him.

If we are not planted until spring, we miss the chance to become firmly rooted in him. It is in October's Spring Garden that we are buried in him, that we may rise again, new and beautiful in him.

In Colossians 3:1-4 Paul gives us these

planting tips for our October Spring Garden:

Planting Tip #1: We must orient our planting areas toward the sun.

When bulbs are planted in the fall, we have to plan for their emergence in the spring. It is the sun's warmth that triggers their new life.

Paul says it this way. **If we wish to flower for Christ, we must orient ourselves toward him.** Our renewing sunlight flows from the One who sits at the right hand of God.

Planting Tip #2: The bulbs must be turned the correct direction.

A bulb is not a ping pong ball. There is a top and a bottom to a bulb. Plant it upside down, and it will try to grow, but it may wither before the shoots can reach the surface.

The same is true for the Christian. **We are rooted in this world, but we must reach out to the Father above.** When our eyes are on him, rather than on the world, we will find the source of our life shining down on us.

Planting Tip #3: Cover the bulbs with plenty of soil.

If the bulbs are only partially buried, and the tops are left exposed to the winter weather, they will die. The storms of winter are too harsh for the tender life that is cocooned within. We must cover the bulbs with soil and mulch them for protection.

Our earthly man is not capable of reaching heaven without God's help. **We cannot live a good enough life, do enough charitable deeds, or write enough checks to make it to heaven.** We must be covered with God, through Christ, who died for us on the cross. Christ is our soil, and the Spirit is our mulch, protecting us from life's storms.

Planting Tip #4: Expect a bountiful display of spring flowers.

The winter is long, but our expectations are high. We anticipate the melting snows, and we watch our beds for the first signs of green. We know what we have prepared, and although our flowerbeds look desolate and forlorn, we are filled with confidence. When spring arrives, our joy will be complete.

In Christ, the expectation of the Church is the same. Life is long, and we have been buried long.

However, when Christ, who is the sunshine that brings us the warmth of life, bursts forth in that final day, we will rise with him in glory, beautiful and brilliant, just as he has planned all along.

When Jesus plants his followers in October's Spring Garden, he plants them just where he needs them. Even though we may only see the darkness of everyday life covering us, Jesus knows what we will look like when we burst forth. He has a master plan.

In summary, when Jesus plants us, he knows what he's doing. When he shines on us, we will bloom for him.

Amen.

Read about it in the Bible:

Colossians 3:1-4 (KJV)

If ye then be risen with Christ, seek those things which are above, where Christ sitteth on the right hand of God. Set your affection on things above, not on things on the earth. For ye are dead, and your life is hid with Christ in God. When Christ, who is our life, shall appear, then shall ye also appear with him in glory.

Planting October's Spring Garden

Questions for Group Discussion

1. How can we plant the seed of Christ's message in our hearts?

   _____

   _____

   _____

2. List the programs your church provides to ensure that children are ministered to.

   _____

   _____

   _____

3. What is a life event that might qualify as a "winter" experience?

   _____

   _____

4. Numerous Bible characters experienced "winter" times in their lives. List three. Include their "winter" challenges.

_____

_____

_____

5. What is a "winter" experience you have gone through? What helped you make it through to the other side?

_____

_____

_____

Scraping the Paint

Colossians 3:5-9

Those of us who are homeowners know the chores of taking care of a house. Plunge this, reattach that, replace all of those, and the list goes on.

One thing we cannot let go is the exterior of our home. Weather beats at the siding, the sun tortures the trim, and any leaks are a disaster in the making.

We have to keep our home in premium condition, if it is to serve us well for a lifetime. One of the most obvious things we can tackle is replacing old, cracked paint with new.

There is a caveat to this, though. **If we simply apply fresh paint to the old,** it will leave cracks and crevasses that can collect dirt and moisture, creating the opportunity for the damage to become greater than before. In addition, **it won't hold. It will crack and peel, sloughing off, leaving the surface uglier than before.**

The solution? Remove all the old paint. We can scrape, apply paint remover, and even sand, but the old paint must come off. Only then will the new paint bond with the wood, becoming a permanent part of the surface.

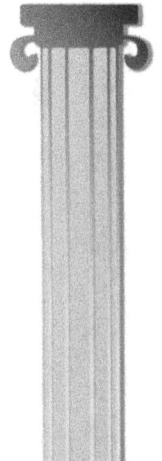

We are like an old house before we come to Christ. We are no longer in premium condition. We are battered with the sins of the world, and they have left their mark on us.

Paul, in Colossians 3:5-9, tells three things we must do, in order that we may become new in Christ.

First, we must scrape the damaged areas.

Scraping the paint on a house is just the first step. It removes the most obvious damage, that paint that is hanging loose, ready to fall away.

Paul says to mortify ourselves. This means to deaden our sensitivity to those things that lead us into sin, especially those involving immorality and passion. In addition, we must learn to put aside greed and the desire for things of this world.

These are the obvious sins, the ones that are easy to see. We must pull out our paint scraper and let those things become no more than crumbling shards of detritus to be swept into the trash bin.

Next, our job is to apply paint remover to the rest.

Once the loose paint is gone, then we get to the stuff that is stuck tight. It must be removed, though, because it will begin to turn loose once we apply the fresh paint, and it will destroy the integrity of the new finish. Only paint remover will take this off.

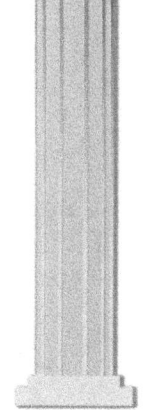

What does Paul encourage us to tackle with our paint remover? What are those sins that are harder to remove?

Anger, getting even with other people, and off-color language. They cling to us like a second skin, and they will destroy the integrity of our walk with Jesus.

Finally, we have to sand the surface smooth.

Scraping can gouge the surface of the wood, and paint remover opens the grain, leaving ridges and valleys that can collect dirt and moisture. Only sanding will smooth these out, creating an ideal surface for our new coat of paint.

How can we sand our earthly man in order to put on the newness of Christ? **Paul says that we are not to lie to one another.** If we do so, we may put on the new paint of Christ, but the surface will be gouged and rough, and the dirt of sin will soon begin to collect on us once more.

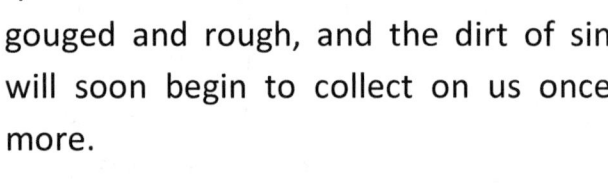

God is our building inspector. He is the one that looks over the job we've done and decides whether we are worth our hire.

God cannot abide sin in any form. When he finds the perfection of Jesus coating our mortal man, he will speak his words of approval unto us, "Well done, my good and faithful servant."

In summary, when we put off the old man, we must scrape and sand to make sure he is completely gone. Only then will Jesus become a permanent part of who we are.

Amen.

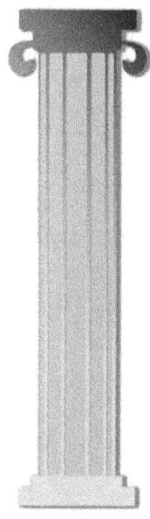

Read about it in the Bible:

Colossians 3:5-9 (KJV)

Mortify therefore your members which are upon the earth; fornication, uncleanness, inordinate affection, evil concupiscence, and covetousness, which is idolatry: For which things' sake the wrath of God cometh on the children of disobedience: In which ye also walked some time, when ye lived in them. But now ye also put off all these; anger, wrath, malice, blasphemy, filthy communication out of your mouth. Lie not one to another, seeing that ye have put off the old man with his deeds;

Scraping the Paint

Questions for Group Discussion

1. Name a godly Bible character that let cracked paint build up in his or her life.

   _____

   _____

   _____

2. Who is a modern minister or evangelist whose cracked paint has been exposed before the world?

   _____

   _____

   _____

3. What is your cracked paint? We all have it, so no hesitation allowed on this question.

   _____

   _____

   _____

4. Christ is our paint remover. List three steps in the spiritual paint removal process.

   _____

   _____

   _____

5. How can we apply a lasting coat of new paint to our Christian walk?

   _____

   _____

   _____

Putting on the Ritz

Colossians 3:10-17

We can all picture a dressy Ritz cracker, round, pierced with multiple holes, and boasting scalloped edges. Lightly browned, they're the best around. However, there are also the Ritz Carlton chain of hotels, the Ritz Camera Store founded in Atlantic City nearly a century ago, and all the other businesses that try to trade off that swanky name.

The term Ritz has come to mean something of higher than average quality.

It also means something to catch the eye; to look flashy; to stand out in a crowd.

Putting on the Ritz is a slang term from as early as 1921, meaning to **dress up and parade oneself at the showiest places around**, whether at the Ritz Hotel in London, or the Ritz-Carlton Hotel at the south end of Central Park. The phrase was so popular it was made into a hit song written and published in 1929 by Irving Berlin. He changed the phrase slightly, dropping the g on the first word, but there was no doubting the reference. It was exactly the same.

They were **"putting on the Ritz."**

When we put on the Ritz, we make ourselves look as fine as possible, showing off the very best we have to offer, making sure everyone notices. We want to be seen.

Christ wants us to "put on the Ritz."

In Colossians 3:10-17, Paul describes our ritzy attire, from our top hats to our highly polished shoes. He makes sure we know the plan, so that we can be the star of the show, the one everyone notices, the standout in the crowd.

Paul lays out a plan for putting on Jesus. He tells us we will look completely different when we are dressed in Jesus, a new man, in fact. People will look for the man we were, and instead, they will find the look of Christ in everything we do and say.

Our new suit of clothes will be that of Christ.

We will be dressed in the finest our Lord has to offer. People will notice, and they will want to join in.

Let's look at our Christ suit:

No. 1: A high hat is first on our agenda.

Otherwise known as a top hat or stove pipe, the high hat is a stunning symbol of status and position. It makes us stand out in the crowd.

However, just as one high hat is the same as another, so we are the same in Jesus. There is no longer Greek nor Jew, circumcision nor uncircumcision, barbarian, Scythian, bond nor free. Rather, Christ is all, and in all.

No. 2: Next comes our narrow collar.

First used by the exclusive Eton College in the 1850s, this iconic style became associated with the school, starting a new trend. Now it is expected in the toniest of situations.

We are the elect of God, exclusive, the toniest of the toney. We must wear our mercy, kindness, humbleness, meekness, and longsuffering, letting them become iconic symbols of Christ in us.

No. 3: A spangled gown or a well-creased tuxedo adds sparkle.

In the Fred Astaire version, these were cutaway daycoats, with striped pants. In any version, we are to wear our very best. For a woman? The glitzier the better, with lots of sparkly doodads.

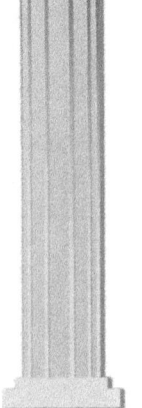

Paul tells us that when we wrap ourselves in the fabric of forgiveness, we have attired ourselves in the most exotic of sartorial creations.

We are to be patient and forgiving with each other, and if anyone tries to quarrel with us, well, we wear the gown of forgiveness, and we are to forgive them, just as Christ forgave us.

No. 4: Silk stockings are a must.

Silk has long been considered the ultimate fabric, soft to the skin, expensive to obtain, and a sign of true affluence and taste.

No one would dress in their best and forget to don stockings. **In the same manner, we cannot forget to put on our charity, which is love for our fellow man.** It is the bond of completion that proves our growth in Christ.

No. 5: Leathers for our feet can't be beat.

In the 1920s, a smooth glossy leather finish became popular. Known as patent leather, it was the stylish way to dress. Slicked down hair, perfectly styled, was the look, and these shoes were an ideal match.

The peace of God is our patent leather finish.

We are to let it rule in our hearts, so

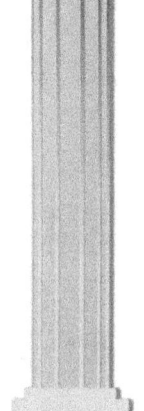

that we are one body in Christ. His peace will smooth our spirits into perfection before the world, enabling us to show our thankfulness in all things.

No. 6: White spats follow.

Spats, or spatterdashes, were designed to keep "spatters" of mud from staining the pant legs. By the twenties, they were a fashion icon, worn for cosmetic reasons, and fashionable for the most upscale dressers, as they covered unsightly laces and fasteners.

Our spatterdashes are the Words of Christ.

When we let the Word dwell in us, teaching and admonishing one another with its wisdom, and incorporating its truth into our songs unto the Lord, no bad thing of this world will stain our Christian experience.

No. 7: We wrap it up with a black tie.

A white tie for day, a black for night. When we don our black tie, we step out into the glitter and pizazz, aiming to see and be seen. Our black tie tells the world so.

Just as our tie is the finishing touch to our fancy dress, so we are to do all things in the name of the Lord Jesus, giving thanks to God and the Father.

Our voices lifted in praise to our heavenly Father become the pièce de résistance that makes our Christ suit complete.

When we "put on the Ritz," people will notice. That is the point, for others to see Christ in us. Let's jazz it up!

In summary, when we put on Christ, the world will want to join our party.

Amen.

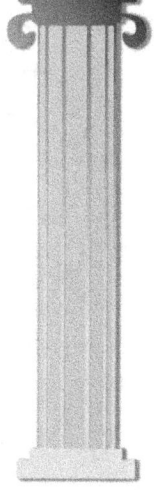

Read about it in the Bible:

Colossians 3:10-17 (KJV)

And have put on the new man, which is renewed in knowledge after the image of him that created him: Where there is neither Greek nor Jew, circumcision nor uncircumcision, Barbarian, Scythian, bond nor free: but Christ is all, and in all. Put on therefore, as the elect of God, holy and beloved, bowels of mercies, kindness, humbleness of mind, meekness, longsuffering; Forbearing one another, and forgiving one another, if any man have a quarrel against any: even as Christ forgave you, so also do ye. And above all these things put on charity, which is the bond of perfectness. And let the peace of God rule in your hearts, to which also ye are called in one body; and be ye thankful. Let the word of Christ dwell in you richly in all wisdom; teaching and admonishing one another in psalms and hymns and spiritual songs, singing with grace in your hearts to the Lord. And whatsoever ye do in word or deed, do all in the name of the Lord Jesus, giving thanks to God and the Father by him.

Putting on the Ritz

Questions for Group Discussion

1. Special clothing is endemic to certain professions. Name a specific profession and the dress we generally associate with it.

   _____

   _____

   _____

2. Putting on the Ritz is about our spiritual clothing. Yet, our outer man must reflect our inner man. What clothing items are a must for a Christian's visual witness?

   _____

   _____

3. How can we "wear" Christ and make him visible to others?

   _____

   _____

4. Come up with three things you can do to non-verbally communicate Christ's love for others.

   _____

   _____

   _____

5. To you, what person most exemplifies the idea of "putting on the Ritz" for Christ? (current or biblical)

   _____

   _____

   _____

The Weaving Machine

Colossians 3:18-25

Fabric does not come from a fabric tree. A woven tapestry does not grow from a tapestry seed, blooming into a beautiful creation on our wall. The coarsest cotton cloth has to be crafted from individual threads, one piece at a time.

Centuries ago, this was done by hand, each layer woven into the whole in a tedious, finger-numbing process that often took weeks to complete. Larger works? The timeframe could run to months or even years.

Today cloth is pumped out on massive weaving machines, giant automated automatons that work tirelessly day and night to produce the intricate fabrics that surround our every waking moment. Without these weaving machines, our lives would be coarser, poorer, and much less enjoyable. Centuries ago we might have owned one set of clothes, been lucky to have a sheet for our mattress, and a towel? Good luck there. Today we have closets stuffed full of textiles that only a king could have afforded in those days.

Our Christian life is one giant tapestry.

Our weaving machine is God the Father in heaven, and we are his threads. He weaves us together in

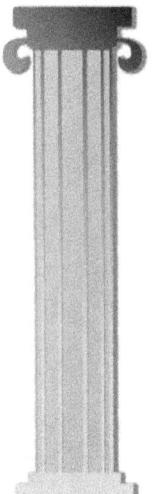

an intricate fashion, choosing just which threads go where, in order to create the most beautiful image possible.

We can see God's weaving machine in action in Colossians 3:18-25. **In this passage, Paul describes each thread in the tapestry and exactly where God needs it to go.**

If we follow God's plan, we will become

beautiful in him.

The Thread of Domestic Life:

In Paul's day and time, women working outside of the home was more unusual than not. What we term "domestic life" was very labor intensive. A woman could not set the dishwasher for midnight, throw in a load of laundry before breakfast, and turn the vacuum on to automatically sweep the floors sometime during the afternoon.

Women were tied to household duties and also to their husbands. Knowing this, Paul instructs wives to submit themselves to their husbands.

However, this by no means suggests lying down and being a doormat.

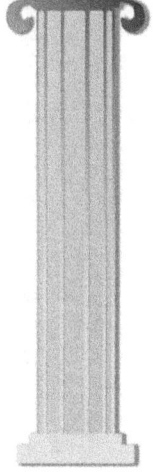

Paul makes this clear when he explains in no uncertain terms that his words are only for those women whose husbands function in the spirit of the Lord.

The Thread Called Husbands:

Husbands and wives were held to

different standards in the 1st century. **A man had rights and privileges that a woman did not possess.** Generally, although there were differences in actual practice, if a man found anything about his wife that was unacceptable, he could divorce her, and once divorced she was branded. No one would marry her.

A wife had no such recourse, except in the most heinous of situations.

Paul compared the love of a husband toward his wife with the love that we offer unto God. We may not agree with God, may even become disgruntled with God, but we do not divorce God. Men are to be the same with their wives. Husbands are not to cast their wives aside carelessly.

We must be there through thick and thin, and it is our love that will smooth the rough places.

The Children Thread:

Children do not grow up with a strong sense of values as an innate and intrinsic part of their core being. Values are not instinctual. They are learned.

The crux is that the values children learn in the home are the same values that transfer to their adult lives and into their relationship with God.

Paul lays out his instructions for children in much the same way as he lays out his instructions for wives. He says, obey your parents in all things. Remember, though, Paul is writing to the church at Colosse, not to a pagan tribe in Britain or North Africa.

When parents function in the spirit of the Lord, they present good models for their children to emulate.

It is pleasing to God when children emulate and obey their parents in all good things.

The Fathers Thread:

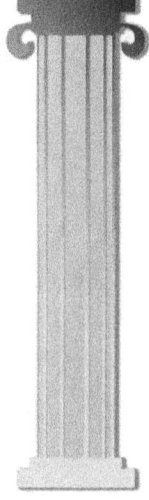

The men of the household had all the power. Legally, men bought and sold, could marry and divorce, and when family property changed hands? The man's fingers were all over it.

Paul does not tell fathers what to do. Culturally, in the timeframe in which Paul wrote this letter, fathers could do almost anything they wanted. Instead, Paul goes at this from a different angle, telling fathers what not to do.

When Paul tells fathers to be careful and not provoke their children to anger, what he is really saying is that we must build our children's respect with love and praise.

If they only fear us, that will transfer into their adult lives, and we will paralyze their effectiveness to the Lord.

The Thread of Servants Everywhere:

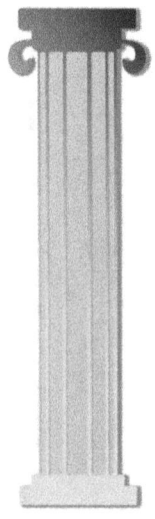

Slavery was a reality in the 1st century, and a portion of those in the Early Church were in legal bondage to other men. Paul did not dispute the realities of his day. Rather, he advised that **even slaves had a duty before the Lord, to present themselves in the light of the teachings of Christ.**

In the modern world, we may not be

legal slaves, but we find ourselves faced with many of the same situations Paul pointed out in this passage. We are not to do our jobs when the boss is watching, but play on our computers when he is away. If we do wrong against our employers, it will come back on us.

We represent Christ, not only in our homes, but in our places of employment, too.

Paul winds up this passage telling us that even as God understands that we all have different roles in life, he does not hold one position up as more important than another. **God does not play favorites, just because one is a wife, a husband, a child, a father, or a slave.** We are all threads in his tapestry.

While we are all made from different threads, **God uses each of us to weave this tapestry of life.** If we play our parts carefully and faithfully, it will be beautiful.

In summary, we are woven into a whole by the hand of Jesus. It is the resulting tapestry that is beautiful.

Amen.

Read about it in the Bible:

Colossians 3:18-25 (KJV)

Wives, submit yourselves unto your own husbands, as it is fit in the Lord. Husbands, love your wives, and be not bitter against them. Children, obey your parents in all things: for this is well pleasing unto the Lord. Fathers, provoke not your children to anger, lest they be discouraged. Servants, obey in all things your masters according to the flesh; not with eye service, as men pleasers; but in singleness of heart, fearing God; And whatsoever ye do, do it heartily, as to the Lord, and not unto men; Knowing that of the Lord ye shall receive the reward of the inheritance: for ye serve the Lord Christ. But he that doeth wrong shall receive for the wrong which he hath done: and there is no respect of persons.

The Weaving Machine

Questions for Group Discussion

1. Picture your parent(s). If married, describe how they interacted with one another. If single, how did he or she interact with you growing up?

   _____

   _____

   _____

2. Is Paul's idea of the husband as the head of the house a product of his day, or is it still current for the 21st century? Why?

   _____

   _____

   _____

3. How can a parent be a Christ-like example to his or her children?

   _____

   _____

4. Who is over you at your place of employment? If you are self-employed, what oversight do you have looking over your shoulder?

   _____

   _____

   _____

5. At this point in your life, what do you think God's role is for you?

   _____

   _____

   _____

Tit for Tat

Colossians 4:1

What goes around comes around; live and let live; do unto others what you would have them do unto you.

These are all phrases for equality; for fair treatment of our fellow man; for living well, yet not living well at another's expense.

Tit for tat. I'll give unto you what you gave unto me.

Normally used in a vindictive mien, this three word phrase's connotation is that

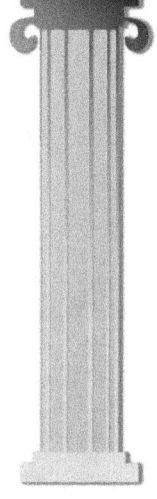

of equivalent retaliation. **Often used in game strategy, it simply means to respond in kind.**

We see this in business with the handshake given in greeting. I reach out—tit—and you reach back—tat—in a warm and congenial manner.

However, if the meeting does not go well, and I treat you unfairly, you are justified in also treating me unfairly.

For example, I strike a fair deal with you, yet months later, I undercut your pricing structure. In tit for tat, you are free to then undercut my pricing structure, and so on.

In true tit-for-tat fashion, I even expect you to do so.

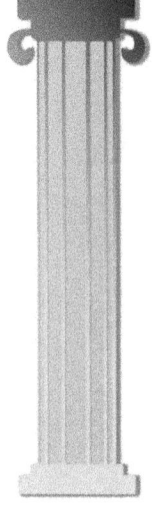

Gas stations do this all the time, one lowering prices, knowing the station on the opposite corner will soon follow suit. And airlines. Anyone who flies frequently is aware of the power of the major players, from baggage fees to food service. Daily fares for every airline can drop radically if only one offers severe discounts.

Tit for tat is biblical, and directly from the mouth of Jesus. We can find his words in Matthew 7:12, Mark 12:31, and Luke 6:31, all telling us to play fairly.

Tit for tat.

Even under the rigid constraints of the Old Covenant, Leviticus 19:18 says not to bear a grudge or take your vengeance on another, but to love that person as you do the one who looks back at you out of the mirror.

Paul addresses this issue very specifically in Colossians 4:1. He is speaking to slave owners, but his words are to us.

The masters of slaves in Paul's day owned them hoof and hind; there were few laws restricting how they were to be treated. Only the most heinous and brutal treatment was condemned.

A Roman slave could not even speak up for himself in a court of law.

Yet Paul encourages tit for tat. Do unto others what you would have them do unto you.

Paul says it this way: **Masters, give unto your servants good and fair treatment . . .**

Yet, those words only give us the tit. Certainly, it is right and good that the master treat his slave well, but where is the benefit for the master?

That brings us to the tat.

Paul continues: **Remember, you also have a master, one who resides in heaven.**

Tit for tat. What goes around comes around. Live a life well-ordered and full of mercy, and let those you interact with each day have the opportunity to live in the same manner. Treat your business partner; your neighbor; your spouse; and your children in the way that you would want to be treated.

The Word of God goes so far as to offer us some suggestions:

Tit for Tat Suggestion #1:

Be positive. Hebrews 10:24.

Tell those around us at least one good thing they've done each day. If they live far away, text it to them.

Tit for Tat Suggestion #2:

Be patient and kind. 1 Corinthians 13:4-7.

Count to three, then don't say it. Then ask if there's anything you can do to help. Then help.

Tit for Tat Suggestion #3:

Show respect. 1 Peter 2:17.

Imagine that the person next to you is your grandmother. How would you treat her?

Tit for Tat Suggestion #4:

Be sympathetic and tenderhearted. 1 Peter 3:8.

Just listen. Then don't offer advice. Listen, cry along, and let them come back and do it again. For free.

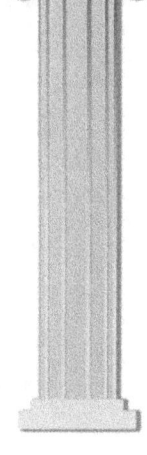

Tit for Tat Suggestion #5:

Be merciful. Ephesians 4:32.

Put on their shoes. Have a meal with them. Get to know the person who's offended you. Then decide if you want to punish them. Finally, remember, you are wearing their shoes.

Tit for Tat Suggestion #6:

Be generous with those in need. 1 John 3:16-19.

Once a month, leave a $50 tip. In ten years, you will not remember, but that waiter always will.

Tit for Tat Suggestion #7:

Honor one another. Romans 12:10.

Cook a cake for a neighbor, simply because they live next door. Meet the postman with a water bottle. Smile, and say, this is because you are special.

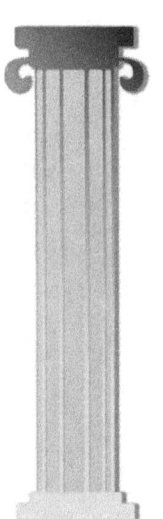

In summary, **if the only rule we live by is the Golden Rule, then we will live well.**

Amen.

Read about it in the Bible:

Colossians 4:1 (KJV)

Masters, give unto your servants that which is just and equal; knowing that ye also have a Master in heaven.

Tit for Tat

Questions for Group Discussion

1. Boys trade hits. Girls trade secrets. What is something you have traded with someone, tit for tat?

   _____

   _____

   _____

2. Does God play tit for tat in our prayers? Why do you think that? Give an example if you can.

   _____

   _____

   _____

3. Give an example of a negative tit-for-tat situation in your life.

   _____

   _____

   _____

4. Now give an example of a time tit for tat generated a positive outcome.

   _____

   _____

   _____

5. Jesus played tit for tat on the cross. His "tit" was his blood on the cross. What is the "tat" he expects from us?

   _____

   _____

   _____

Broken Rope

Colossians 4:2-6

The Inca Empire in Central and South America was at its height 500 years ago. It had a rich oral language still spoken today by about a third of the Peruvian population. Yet, little is known about the specifics of how the government was set up or its power disseminated.

The Inca had no written language.

What they did have was quipu, a coded system of knotted ropes for recording vital knowledge and other important information. This information could be carried over vast distances or stored for later reference without the possibility of misinterpretation.

Facts were recorded in the rope, from tax obligations, census records, and calendric information, to military organization, vital to maintaining political control. The knots were easily read and provided invaluable record-keeping for a vast empire—as long as the rope remained unbroken.

What did a broken rope mean? Miscommunication, invalid information, and a decline of trust in the truth. A broken rope was a disaster in the making.

We have knotted ropes of our own. They are called prayer. They stretch between us and God, the series of knots recording our communication with him.

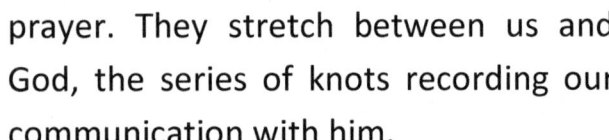

Paul encourages us not to let our ropes become broken. We must maintain a solid line of prayer, making it a regular habit for every believer.

Paul describes six vital knots on our prayer rope in Colossians 4:2-6:

Knot #1: The Knot of Thanksgiving

Verse 2 describes the way we should present our prayers to the Father. We must come first with thanksgiving, for when we show our appreciation to the One who gives us life, we stir his heart towards us. We become tightly knotted with him, bound together, and in one accord.

Knot #2: The Knot of Pastoral Support

Verse 3 encourages us to support those in direct ministry over us. It is through our pastors and lay ministers that God reveals his mysteries unto us. Without our prayers, our leaders cannot stand firm in the face of the evil one, and their knots will unravel to become loose fibers blowing in the wind.

Knot #3: The Knot of Christ

Verse 4 is the core tenant of our faith. If we do not preach Christ as the Truth, the Light, and the Way, all else is for nothing. Without this knot, all we hold in our hands is broken rope.

Knot #4: The Knot of Wisdom

Verse 5 starts with an admonition that we pay attention to how we appear to others. We have to "order our behavior" in such a way that those who are not a part of our faith see Christ in us. In 1 Corinthians 10:23 Paul states that everything is permitted, but everything is not beneficial. Romans 14:13 says not to be a stumbling block with our behavior. We must be the tight knot that does not unravel or break.

Knot #5: The Knot of Time

Verse 5 ends with an instruction to use our time for the furthering of the gospel of Christ. We must be diligent in recognizing the opportunities 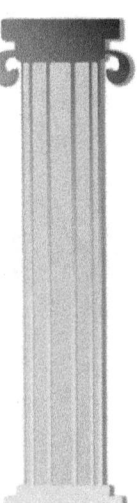 Christ presents unto us to share with those who do not know him. When we put the message of the cross above our own needs, we will see ministry opportunities in every doorway and on every street corner, reinforcing our rope of communication with the Father.

Knot #6: The Knot of Speech

Verse 6 reminds us that our speech is

our spoken presentation of the Christ who lives in us. When we are gracious and pleasant, and we speak regularly of the evidence of Christ in us, we will be able to minister to others, because they will trust in our unbroken rope.

Today, quipu is rarely used in the lands of the old Inca Empire. When it is, it is mostly for ceremonial use, not for recording and conveying important information. **The true quipu, buried with the dead and unused for centuries, now crumbles at the slightest touch, nothing more than broken rope.** It no longer carries the power of an empire in its fibers.

What we do not use, we lose. **We must pray on a regular basis, keeping our prayer ropes stretched taut, so that our knots never crumble.** Only then will we continue in the true power of our Lord.

In summary, when we do not pray, our power that comes through Christ becomes frayed, no more than old, broken rope.

Amen.

Read about it in the Bible:

Colossians 4:2-6 (KJV)

Continue in prayer, and watch in the same with thanksgiving; Withal praying also for us, that God would open unto us a door of utterance, to speak the mystery of Christ, for which I am also in bonds: That I may make it manifest, as I ought to speak. Walk in wisdom toward them that are without, redeeming the time. Let your speech be always with grace, seasoned with salt, that ye may know how ye ought to answer every man.

Broken Rope

Questions for Group Discussion

1. Write down a strong memory you have of someone no longer living. Is it an action or something they wrote that you remember?

   _____

   _____

   _____

2. What is something you did for someone else that made a huge impact on you?

   _____

   _____

   _____

3. Broken Rope is all about action. Name something you can do for a specific person that will make a significant impact on his or her life.

   _____

   _____

4. Time is a knot on our rope. How can you make more time for others in your life?

   _____

   _____

   _____

5. List three people you intend to give additional time to. How will you do this?

   _____

   _____

   _____

Refer-a-Friend

Colossians 4:7-14

Win a $10 gift card! All we have to do is refer a friend to the latest sales program. Netflix will give us a month free for every friend we refer. Dropbox? Extra cloud storage space. Scottrade? Free online stock market trades. Online gaming? Points, bonus levels, and extra lives.

Friend referrals are one of the most beneficial ways of advertising that any company can use. It's free, it's sincere, and most of all, there is an emotional link between the friend and the product. The interest in the product comes from the connection with the friend, and because of that, it is stronger, even before the product has actually changed hands.

In a job interview, we call this a letter of recommendation. Without one, that job offer may evaporate with our first interview question. With one, we are a shoo-in for the position.

Paul understood this implicitly. He knew that tapping his network of friendships and associations would spread the gospel faster and farther than if unknown people carried the story of Christ, no matter how enthusiastic their message.

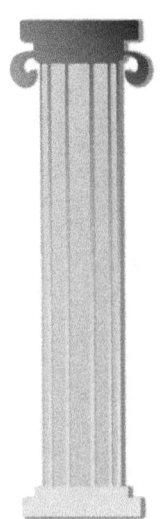

In the book of Colossians, Paul writes to a church he has never visited. They are being led astray by false teachings.

Paul knows people who can steer them the right direction, so he refers those friends to the church at Colosse.

We can read his recommendations in Colossians 4:7-14. Let's look at the people in Paul's Refer-a-Friend program:

Tychicus

Paul uses two words to describe Tychicus: beloved and faithful.

Tychicus was particularly valued by Paul. He served as Paul's courier, hand delivering letters and messages, and fielding questions from other churches about Paul's imprisonment.

Onesimus

Paul uses the same two words to describe Onesimus: beloved and faithful.

However, Onesimus carries a special recommendation. Onesimus is a runaway slave who has come to know Christ as his savior. Paul especially treasured Onesimus, and he desired Onesimus' brotherhood in Christ to supersede his position as a runaway slave.

Aristarchus

Paul describes Aristarchus as his fellow prisoner.

Aristarchus, a Greek from Thessalonica, is also mentioned in various verses in Acts and in the book of Philemon. After a rough time at Ephesus, Aristarchus accompanied Paul in his travels to Macedonia and Palestine, and later to Rome. Aristarchus was Paul's right arm.

Marcus

Paul gives Marcus his highest praise.

Marcus, or John Mark, had once been at odds with Paul, causing a rift between Paul and his companion Barnabas so great that the men never ministered together again. However, Marcus soon rose to meet Paul's expectations, eventually penning the gospel of Mark in the New Testament.

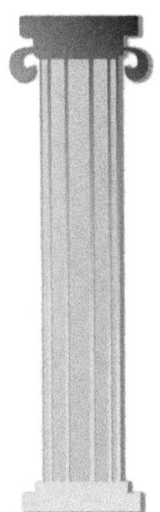

Jesus, called Justus

Paul includes Jesus, called Justus, in his most select circle of friends.

Paul names Jesus Justus as a fellow Jew, one of three, including Aristarchus and Mark, who have been a comfort to him. Jesus, also called the Christ, came first to the Jews, and those of the Jewish faith who found their hope in Jesus Christ were especially treasured by Paul.

Epaphras

Paul calls Epaphras a servant of Christ.

In Paul's eyes, there was no greater honor to bestow on a fellow believer. Epaphras was a mighty prayer warrior, conspicuous in his perseverance for Christ. Epaphras carried a zeal for the spiritual welfare of others.

Luke

Luke, a great friend of Paul, the writer of the third canonical gospel, needs no introduction to the modern church.

In the same vein, Paul's referral gives little information about his friend, other than to describe him as a beloved physician. The bond between the two men was evidently well-known. This is the same Luke who was with Paul during his last days at Mamertine prison in Rome, where Paul wrote his second and fi-

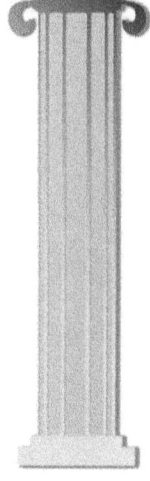

nal missive to Timothy.

Demas

Demas faithfully served alongside Paul in Rome, and Paul recommends him to the body at Colosse.

However, later, in 2 Timothy, Paul would reveal Demas' desertion from Paul's ministry. He makes it clear that following Christ is a choice. Comfort and wealth meant more to Demas than the advancement of the gospel of Christ. Demas becomes Paul's greatest disappointment and most heart-felt failure.

Paul opened the doors of Colosse to these men. His letter of recommendation put them in the enviable position of not having to prove themselves to the believers there.

These were men who had already proved themselves to the Lord.

In summary, when God knows he can trust us, he will recommend us to the people of the world.

Amen.

Read about it in the Bible:

Colossians 4:7-14 (KJV)

All my state shall Tychicus declare unto you, who is a beloved brother, and a faithful minister and fellowservant in the Lord: Whom I have sent unto you for the same purpose, that he might know your estate, and comfort your hearts; With Onesimus, a faithful and beloved brother, who is one of you. They shall make known unto you all things which are done here. Aristarchus my fellow prisoner saluteth you, and Marcus, sister's son to Barnabas, (touching whom ye received commandments: if he come unto you, receive him;) And Jesus, which is called Justus, who are of the circumcision. These only are my fellow workers unto the kingdom of God, which have been a comfort unto me. Epaphras, who is one of you, a servant of Christ, saluteth you, always laboring fervently for you in prayers, that ye may stand perfect and complete in all the will of God. For I bear him record, that he hath a great zeal for you, and them that are in Laodicea, and them in Hierapolis. Luke, the beloved physician, and Demas, greet you.

Refer-a-Friend

Questions for Group Discussion

1. Have you ever written a job reference for someone? If someone wrote one for you, what positive things might it say?

   _____

   _____

   _____

2. List your qualifications for leading your body's Sunday evening service. Don't be modest.

   _____

   _____

   _____

3. Think of another member of your body. What are his or her qualifications for leading the Sunday evening service?

   _____

   _____

4. Think of someone you know who has left the church. Why do you think they no longer follow after Christ?

_____

_____

_____

5. Paul was a missionary, of sorts. Yet, he never knew Christ in person. What made him especially qualified to present the gospel?

_____

_____

_____

Tarmac Touchdown

Colossians 4:15-18

Airlines depend on repeat business. Flyers have a multitude of choices, and for that reason, it is important to wind down each and every flight on an upbeat note.

It is vital to the success of the airline company to have a good tarmac touchdown. The wheels must be lowered at just the right time, the airplane must be angled correctly, and the smoother the contact with the runway, the more positive each passenger's memory of the flight will be.

The pilot's skill will be admired, and the compliments will flow like warm honey. The turbulence at 35,000 feet won't be forgotten, nor will the baby that cried for two hours. Yet, we will be satisfied.

The ending always flavors the beginning, and a pleasing tarmac touchdown will coat everything else on the flight with pleasing overtones.

Paul was winding down his letter to the believers at Colosse. He hadn't been able to avoid turbulence, either, for there were issues he'd addressed head on. **Yet, he understood the importance of a smooth and uneventful tarmac touchdown, that if his letter closed on a smooth and upbeat note, his readers would accept everything else he'd said more graciously.**

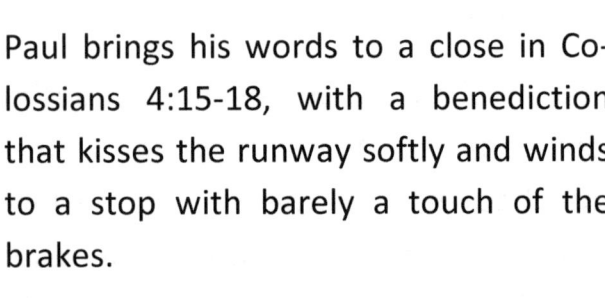

Paul brings his words to a close in Colossians 4:15-18, with a benediction that kisses the runway softly and winds to a stop with barely a touch of the brakes.

Verse 15: **Paul lowers the wheels.**

Lowering the craft's wheels is vital to landing an airplane. It is a preparatory step, readying the craft for those to come. Without this pivotal step in the landing process, nothing else will be successful.

Paul lowers his wheels by greeting a nearby church, one that might also read his epistle. He mentions Nymphas, who hosts the church in his home, by name.

Verse 16: **He kisses the pavement.**

When the wheels touch the tarmac, that contact is felt throughout the entire craft. Reality has met reality, and everyone knows.

The reality is that the letter to the Colossians will be read by other believers. Paul encourages this. He tells the believers at Colosse to share their letter with the Laodiceans, and to also read the epistle from Laodicea.

Verse 17: **He applies the brakes.**

An aircraft cannot coast to a stop. If a pilot takes his hands and feet off the controls once contact is made with the ground, expecting the plane to make it safely to the terminal on its own, it will veer off the runway. It will not reach its final destination.

Paul cautions Archippus, a man thought to be the son of Philemon, and perhaps the pastor of the church at Colosse, to take heed to the direction of his ministry. God needed him to reach the terminal, not veer off the runway.

Verse 18: **He thanks his passengers for flying with him.**

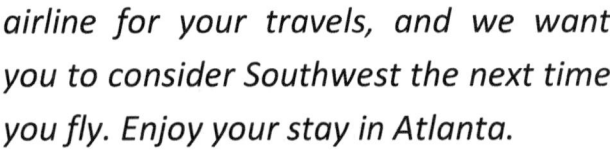

The final words of a flight are the ones that stay with us. For example: *Thank you for flying with Southwest Airlines. We know you can choose any airline for your travels, and we want you to consider Southwest the next time you fly. Enjoy your stay in Atlanta.*

Paul thanks his readers for bearing with him, asks them to keep him in mind when they pray, and encourages them to enjoy their walk in the gospel.

Repeat business. A multitude of choices. A good tarmac touchdown. Paul, a master orator and writer, covered all the bases. Today, we return to his words on a weekly basis. We look past the Qur'an, the Book of Mormon, and the Writings of Bahá'u'lláh.

From our multitude of choices, we pick up the Bible, becoming repeat business for Paul's writings.

It is when we accept the message he brings us that our tarmac touchdown is complete, for the message becomes real in our hearts.

In summary, it is our connection with Jesus that makes our lives real, and we find that when we read his Word.

Amen.

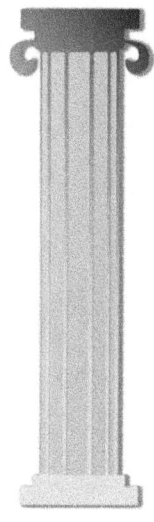

Read about it in the Bible:

Colossians 4:15-18 (KJV)

Salute the brethren which are in Laodicea, and Nymphas, and the church which is in his house. And when this epistle is read among you, cause that it be read also in the church of the Laodiceans; and that ye likewise read the epistle from Laodicea. And say to Archippus, Take heed to the ministry which thou hast received in the Lord, that thou fulfill it. The salutation by the hand of me Paul. Remember my bonds. Grace be with you. Amen.

Tarmac Touchdown

Questions for Group Discussion

1. How do your church leaders greet the body at the end of each service?

   _____

   _____

   _____

2. People who have never met you still have contact with you through social media. What social media have you been in or a part of? (newspapers, pictures, online websites, yearbooks)

   _____

   _____

   _____

3. How do you greet people at the end of each church service?

   _____

   _____

4. If you were to caution your pastor, what would you say to him or her?

_____

_____

_____

5. Write in the space below an encouraging benediction that you can repeat to every person you greet in your church body. This will become how people think of you, so make it good.

_____

_____

_____

Look for these additional topics on the MyChurchNotes.net website:

2 Timothy
Beatitudes
Discipleship
Evangelism
Faith
Family
Healing
Hope
Kingdom of God
Money
Prayer
Relationships
Repentance
Salvation
Worship

MyChurchNotes.net is a faith-based ministry founded on a belief in the Father, the Son, and the Holy Spirit. All MyChurchNotes.net articles are based on Scripture and created especially for MyChurchNotes.net.

Our Mission Statement is to take the Word of God into all the nations, and proclaim that he is Lord!

If you enjoyed
Understanding Paul's Epistle to the Colossians,
please visit us at our website:

www.MyChurchNotes.net

We look forward to hearing from you.

Website and Publication Powered by:

Bright Herd . . . for All Your Website and Media Design Needs.
www.brightherd.com
contact@brightherd.com

www.ingramcontent.com/pod-product-compliance
Lightning Source LLC
LaVergne TN
LVHW051830080426
835512LV00018B/2807